WALDORF EDUCATION
AND ANTHROPOSOPHY

1

[XIII]

FOUNDATIONS OF WALDORF EDUCATION

RUDOLF STEINER

Waldorf Education and Anthroposophy 1

Nine Public Lectures

FEBRUARY 23, 1921 – SEPTEMBER 16, 1922

Anthroposophic Press

The publisher wishes to acknowledge the inspiration and support of Connie and Robert Dulaney

❖ ❖ ❖

This volume is a translation of *Erziehungs- und Unterrichtsmethoden auf anthro-posophischer Grundlage,* which is vol. 304 of the Complete Centenary Edition of the works of Rudolf Steiner, published by Rudolf Steiner Nachlassverwaltung, Dornach, Switzerland, 1979.

Published by Anthroposophic Press
834 Main Street, PO Box 358
Spencertown, New York 12165
www.steinerbooks.org

ISBN 978-1-62148-369-4

Printed in the United States of America

Contents

Introduction

This book contains a collection of public lectures given in 1921–1922 by Rudolf Steiner on educational and social questions. It is presented here for the first time in English and contains a number of surprising jewels not found anywhere else.

The year 1921 proved to be a most eventful time in the life of the anthroposophical movement. The First World War had ended and conditions were stabilizing, though in middle Europe many social problems still remained. Rudolf Steiner had spent most of the war years in Dornach, Switzerland, and although he had given a number of lectures in Switzerland and Germany, it had not been possible for him to visit other countries.

One of his first extensive journeys abroad took him to the Netherlands for a two-and-a-half-week lecture tour. In addition to lectures to members, he gave a number of presentations to a wider public.

The first of these lectures, given in the Hague, deals directly with the Guardian of the Threshold, the spiritual being who separates our ordinary consciousness from our spiritual consciousness. Without any introduction, Rudolf Steiner embarks upon basic questions regarding the materialistic age we live in and the dawning of a new, supersensible consciousness. His remarks are full of telling examples and analogies. The task of spiritual science is to help modern humanity, strongly affected by scientific training, to cross the threshold into a supersensible dimension by fully conscious means. Steiner argues persuasively that these considerations are of vital importance for understanding the pedagogical needs of our time.

The second lecture deals more specifically with the urgent need to recognize the developmental stages of the child, addressing the question of a curriculum that meets the needs of children. It emphasizes Steiner's high regard for the results of scientific research and the achievements of medical science. Spiritual science does not seek to diminish the contributions of prevailing materialistic views but rather to add a further dimension to them so that the human being can again be understood to consist of body, soul, and spirit.

The two public lectures given in Switzerland on September 26 and November 11 provide us with a vivid picture of how Rudolf Steiner dealt with a public hardly conversant with the new ideals of education. Any reader—from layperson to parent to teacher—can gain an enormous amount from these presentations, for Rudolf Steiner also discusses what is meant by healthy and unhealthy attitudes toward the growing child. The words of Goethe are quoted: "Consider the *what*, but pay even more attention to the *how*." Steiner shows little interest for rigid educational principles and methods, but urges instead that the teacher practice an art of education based on insight into the nature of the growing child. He recommends that all teachers study Schiller's central work, *Letters on the Aesthetic Education of Man*, stating that they would gain considerably from doing so. Again and again, the three phases of the development of the child—imitation, authority, and freedom—are dealt with in an inspiring manner.

The single public lectures on education were given in Oslo, during a visit Steiner made to Scandinavia. An interesting theme, which Steiner spoke of in earlier lectures to members of the Anthroposophical Society, emerges here. In order to educate children rightly, we should discover the element of "unbornness." Steiner coined this term to express that we should form a relationship with what the human being experiences in the spiritual world before birth. For thousands of years humanity has been concerned with "immortality." Now, in the new age of light, the concept of "unbornness" should be added, so that we develop a devotional understanding of what children bring with them.

Of the twelve trips abroad that Rudolf Steiner made during the year 1922, special reference should be made to his stay in England from April 14–25. Well-known educators, such as Professor Millicent Mackenzie, at that time Professor of Education at University College, Cardiff, Wales, were active members of the committee that promoted the lectures Rudolf Steiner gave in Oxford in August 1922.[1] Professor Mackenzie had attended the Christmas course for teachers at the Goetheanum in 1921,[2] and had been so impressed that, after the Oxford lectures, she invited Rudolf Steiner to lecture on education in connection with the Shakespeare festival in Stratford-on-Avon. As a result of these presentations, Professor Mackenzie and Principal L.P. Jacks, then head of Manchester College, sponsored what proved to be a breakthrough for the Waldorf impulse in England.

The festival at Stratford-on-Avon, which was to prove so fruitful, began on April 18 with lectures by some distinguished representatives of British intellectual life, dealing with Shakespeare's work. The conference, arranged by the committee working for "New Ideals in Education," was set at the very center of this festivity. The two lectures Steiner gave in Stratford appear in this collection. In addition to studying these texts, it may be

---

1. Published as *The Spiritual Ground of Education* (London: Anthroposophical Publishing Co., 1947) (GA305 in the Collected Works).
2. Published as *Soul Economy and Waldorf Education.* (Spring Valley, NY: Anthroposophic Press, 1986) (GA303 in the Collected Works).

of interest to hear what Steiner himself later reported about this Shakespeare festival:

> In this connection I was permitted to state my anthroposophical point of view regarding Shakespeare, education, and the requirements of the spiritual life today. One of the ways in which the educational power of Shakespeare's art is involved in the history of human evolution is through the influence that Shakespeare's art exerted upon Goethe. The question must be asked: Upon what does this tremendous influence rest?
>
> When I ask myself this question, I am confronted by a fact in supersensible experience. Anyone who is in a position to devote himself livingly to Shakespeare's dramas and then carry this experience into that world which spreads out before 'exact clairvoyance' can find that the figures of Shakespeare's dramas continue to appear before the soul in the supersensible realm as living, whereas the figures out of the new naturalistic dramas are either transformed completely through this process into puppets or, in a sense, become immobile. In imagination, Shakespeare's figures continue to live. They do not continue to carry out the same actions as in the dramas; rather, they act in different situations and with a changed course of factual events. I believe this indicates that Shakespeare's figures are deeply rooted in the spiritual world, and that Goethe, in his devotion to Shakespearean drama, unconsciously experienced this fact of their being deeply rooted. When he turned to Shakespeare, Goethe felt as if he himself were seized upon by events of the spirit world. I had this experience in the back of my mind when I had the opportunity to speak in Stratford about Shakespeare, Goethe, and the nature of education in three lectures. My

> conviction of this was especially vivid when I spoke on April 23, the real Shakespeare Day, about 'Shakespeare and the New Ideals.'
>
> The programs arranged by the committee for 'New Ideals in Education' were accompanied by presentations of Shakespeare dramas in the Shakespeare Memorial Theatre. We had the opportunity to see *Othello*, *Julius Caesar*, *The Taming of the Shrew*, *Twelfth Night*, *All's Well that Ends Well*, and *Much Ado about Nothing*.
>
> The presentation of the comedies was satisfying, but I have a different conception of the right presentation of the tragedies.

An anecdote, recorded by Harry Collison,[3] could be added for local color: "Every evening the party went to performances of Shakespeare's plays. In *Twelfth Night* when Sir Toby Belch sat on the lap of Andrew Aguecheek, Rudolf Steiner was taken by such a laughing fit that the audience turned round and the performers themselves burst out laughing, hardly able to contain themselves."

Newspaper reports indicated the importance of the Shakespeare festival and the conference on education. Rudolf Steiner made a marked impression on the public and the report from the *London Times* of April 29 bears this out.

> The famous person in this year's conference was Dr. Rudolf Steiner, who is distinguished at present not only in the field of education but also in other fields. In the light of spiritual science, he gives new forces of life to a number

3. Collison (1868–1945), a lawyer, painter, and writer, was a student of Rudolf Steiner from 1910. Authorized by Rudolf Steiner to translate his works into English, Collison founded the Anthroposophical Publishing Company. From 1923, he was the General Secretary of the English Anthroposophical Society.

> of dogmas hitherto held in check, and he promises to teachers relief from unnecessary difficulty through learning to know the soul of the child with the help of supersensible knowledge.... Speaking in the German language, Dr. Steiner was able to hold his audience in an extraordinary manner, in spite of the interpretation interjected after each twenty minutes, as he presented statements regarding the spiritual-scientific school in Dornach, Switzerland, and his own researches regarding the nature of man.

During this period, spiritual science experienced a considerable breakthrough. The first Waldorf school, founded in Stuttgart in September, 1919, was flourishing, and seeds had been planted for similar schools in Holland and England. Rudolf Steiner was able to present his work before crowded auditoriums in the greatest cities of middle Europe.

At the West/East Conference in Vienna, he addressed more than two hundred people for twelve consecutive evenings. The lectures were reported daily in the local press.[4]

In September, a course was given in Dornach mainly for French participants. The lectures have been printed under the title *Philosophy, Cosmology and Religion.*[5] This very special event also brought about the reconciliation between Edouard Schuré[6]

---

4. See *The Tension between East and West* (Anthroposophic Press: Spring Valley, NY:, 1983).
5. Anthroposophic Press: Spring, Valley, NY, 1986.
6. Schuré (1841–1929), French mystic, writer, and friend of Rudolf Steiner, was the author of, among others, *Richard Wagner, son oeuvre et son ideé* (1875), *The Great Initiates* (1889), *Les Femmes Inspiratrices, L'Evolution Divine,* and the dramas *The Children of Lucifer* and *The Mystery of Eleusis.* Marie von Sivers (later Steiner) had known Schuré before the end of the nineteenth century and later translated some of his works into German. Rudolf Steiner and Schuré first met in May 1906.

and Steiner. They had become estranged during the First World War because of the strong patriotism of Schuré, who like many Alsatians had bitterly resented the German annexation of their province in 1871. The meeting of the eighty-one-year-old Schuré, the renowned author, with the sixty-one-year-old Steiner was the warmest possible. Rudolf Steiner prepared a daily outline for Jules Sauerwein, the most prominent French journalist of his time, who acted as translator. In the present collection of public lectures we shall find Rudolf Steiner's own report of a lecture on education, which he gave during the French course. It has the crispness of a statement that would appeal particularly to the French mind.

It should perhaps be mentioned that the present collection of lectures given in different parts of Europe also very much reflects the mentality and the interest of each different nation.

Finally, the publishers should be thanked for making available in English, after so many years, a collection of lectures that can help particularly parents and teachers to gain a clearer picture of how to address a wider public on the central questions of a spiritual-scientifically oriented education. Much can be learned from them, for they are totally uncompromising, although never intended to distress an unprepared audience with a terminology that would be obscure or inappropriate. These lectures could well be placed also in the hands of beginners who wish to find out in a succinct and clear way what Waldorf education is really about.

R. M. Querido, LLD
Boulder, Colorado

1

Anthropospophical Spiritual Science and the Great Questions of our Present Civilization

THE HAGUE — FEBRUARY 23, 1921

Anyone who chooses to address the themes that I shall address tonight and again on the 27th knows that many people today long for a new element in contemporary spiritual life, an impulse that could revitalize and transform important aspects of our present civilization. Such longings live especially in those who try to look deeply into their own inner being, stirred by the various signs in contemporary society indicating that, unless present trends change, our civilization is heading for a general collapse. These signs themselves, of course, are a result of many characteristic features of the cultural stream of Western Europe over the last few centuries.

What may be said about the supersensible worlds today may therefore be said to every human soul. It may be said even to a hermit, a recluse, who has withdrawn from the world. Above all, however, it may be said to those who stand fully and firmly in life: for what we are talking about is every human being's concern.

But this is not the only point of view from which I wish to speak today and again on the 27th. I want to talk about how, if we let them work upon our souls, the fundamental issues facing our civilization affect our attitudes. Those who feel called upon to lead their fellow human beings will find much that is inwardly disturbing here and much that makes them yearn for a renewal of certain aspects of spiritual and cultural life.

If we consider humanity's present cultural, spiritual situation, we may trace it back to two fundamental issues. One shines out in contemporary science and in the way in which scientific life has developed during the last three or four hundred years. The other shines out from the practical sphere of life, which, naturally, has been largely influenced by modern science.

To begin with, let us look at what science has brought in its wake more recently. At this point, to avoid any misunderstanding, let me state clearly that anthroposophical spiritual science—as I shall represent it here—must in no way be thought of as opposing the spirit of modern science, whose triumphant and important successes the exponents of spiritual science fully recognize. Precisely because it wishes to enter without prejudice into the spirit of natural science, anthroposophical spiritual science must go beyond its confines and objectives. Natural science, with its scrupulous, specialized disciplines, provides exact, reliable information about much in our human environment. But, when a human soul asks about its deepest, eternal being, it receives no answer from natural science, least of all when science searches in all honesty and without prejudice. This is why we find many people today who out of an inner religious need—in some cases more, in others less—long for a renewal of the old ways of looking at the world.

The outer sciences, and anthropology in particular, already draw our attention to the fact that our forebears, centuries ago, knew nothing of what splits and fragments many souls today; namely, the disharmony between scientific knowledge on one hand and religious experience on the other. If we compare our situation today with what prevailed in ancient times, we find that the leaders of humanity who cultivated science then—however childlike their science might appear to us now—also kindled the religious spirit of their people. There was certainly no split between these two spiritual streams.

Today, many souls long for the return of something similar. Yet one cannot say that a renewal of ancient forms of wisdom—whether Chaldean, Egyptian, Indian, or any other—would benefit our present society. Those who advocate such a return can hardly be said to understand the significance of human evolution, for they overlook its real mission. They do not recognize that it is impossible today to tread the same spiritual paths that were trodden thousands of years ago. It is an intrinsic feature of human evolution that every age should have its own particular character. In every age, people must seek inner fulfillment or satisfaction in appropriate though distinctly different ways. Because we live and are educated in the twentieth century, our soul life today needs something different from what people living in distant antiquity once needed for their souls. A renewal of ancient attitudes toward the world would hardly benefit our present time, although knowledge of them could certainly help in finding our bearings. Familiarizing ourselves with such attitudes could also help us recognize the source of inner satisfaction in ancient times. Now, this inner satisfaction or fulfillment was, in fact, the result of a relationship to scientific knowledge fundamentally different from what we experience today.

There is a certain phenomenon to which I would like to draw your attention. To do so is to open myself to the accusation of being either paradoxical or downright fantastical. However, one can say many things today that, even a few years ago, would have been highly dangerous to mention because of the situation that prevailed then. The last few catastrophic years

[1914–1918] have brought about a change in people's thinking and feeling about such things. Compared with the habits of thought and feeling of the previous decade, people today are readier to accept the idea that the deepest truths might at first strike one as being paradoxical or even fantastical.

In the past, people spoke of something that today—especially in view of our scientific knowledge—would hardly be acceptable. This is something that will be discussed again in a relatively short time, probably even in educated, cultured circles. I refer to the Guardian of the Threshold.[1] This guardian stands between the ordinary world of the senses, which forms the firm ground of orthodox science and is where we lead our daily lives, and those higher worlds in which the supersensible part of the human being is integrated into the spiritual world. Between the sensory world—whose phenomena we can observe and in which we can recognize the working of natural laws with our intellect—and that other world to which we belong with our inner being, between these two worlds, the ancients recognized an abyss. To attain true knowledge, they felt, that abyss had first to be crossed. But only those were allowed to do so who had undergone intensive preparation under the guidance of the leaders of the mystery centers. Today, we have a rather different view of what constitutes adequate preparation for a scientific training and for living in a scientific environment. In ancient times, however, it was firmly believed that an unprepared candidate could not possibly be allowed to receive higher knowledge of the human being. But why should this have been the case?

---

1. A literary source for this designation is Bulwer Lytton's *Zanoni*. See also, among others, Rudolf Steiner: *How to Know Higher Worlds*, chapter 10; *Occult Science*, chapter 3; the Mystery Drama, *The Guardian of the Threshold*, and *A Road to Self Knowledge and The Threshold of the Spiritual World.*

An answer to that question can be found only if insight is gained into the development of the human soul during the course of evolution. Such insight goes beyond the limits of ordinary historical research. Basically, present historical knowledge draws only on external sources and disregards the more subtle changes that the human psyche undergoes.[2]

For instance, we do not usually take into account the particular condition of soul of those ancient peoples who were rooted in the primeval oriental wisdom of their times, decadent forms of which only survive in the East today. Fundamentally speaking, we do not realize how differently such souls were attuned to the world. In those days, people already perceived external nature through their senses as we do today. To a certain extent, they also combined all of the various sense impressions with their intellect. But, in doing so, they did not feel themselves separated from their natural surroundings. They still perceived an element of soul and spirit within themselves. They felt their physical organization permeated by soul and spirit. At the same time, they also experienced soul and spirit in lightning and in thunder, in drifting clouds, in stones, plants, and beasts. What they could divine within themselves, they could also feel out in nature and in the entire universe. To these human beings of the past, the whole universe was imbued with soul and spirit.

On the other hand, they lacked something that we, today, possess to a marked degree, that is, they did not have as pronounced and intensive a self-consciousness as we do. Their self-awareness was dimmer and dreamier than ours today. That was

---

2. For Steiner's approach to the evolution of consciousness, see Stewart Easton, *Man and World in the Light of Anthroposophy* (Anthroposophic Press: Hudson, NY, 1989) Chapter 2; also Rudolf Steiner (among others): *Egyptian Myths and Mysteries*; *Turning Points in Spiritual History*; *The East in the Light of the West* and *The Archangel Michael: His Mission and Ours*. (For bibliographic information, see Bibliography).

still the case even in ancient Greece. Whoever imagines that the condition of soul—the psychic organization—of the ancient Greeks was more or less the same as our own can understand only the later stages of Greek culture. During its earlier phases, the state of the human soul was not the same as it is today, for in those days there still existed a dim awareness of humanity's kinship with nature. Just as a finger, if endowed with some form of self awareness, would feel itself to be a part of the whole human organism and could not imagine itself leading a separate existence—for then it would simply wither away—so the human being of those early times felt closely united with nature and certainly not separate from it.[3]

The wise leaders of the ancient mystery schools believed that this awareness of humanity's connection with nature represented the moral element in human self-consciousness, which must never be allowed to conceive of the world as being devoid of soul and spirit. They felt that if the world were to be conceived of as being without soul and spirit—as has now happened in scientific circles and in our daily lives—human souls would be seized by a kind of faintness. The teachers of ancient wisdom foresaw that faintness or swooning of the soul would occur if people adopted the kind of world-view we have today.

You might well wonder what the justification for saying such things is. To illustrate that there is a justification, I would like to take an example from history—just one out of many others that could have been chosen.

Today, we feel rightfully satisfied with the generally accepted system of the universe that no longer reflects what the eye can observe outwardly in the heavens, as it still did in the Middle

---

3. For a more extended treatment of the relation of Greek thought to the ancient mystery schools, see "The Mission of the Archangel Michael," lecture 4, in *The Archangel Michael: His Mission and Ours.*

Ages. We have adopted the Copernican view of the universe, which is a heliocentric one. During the Middle Ages, however, people believed that the earth rested in the center of the planetary system—in fact, in the center of the entire starry world—and that the sun, together with the other stars, revolved around the earth. The heliocentric system of the universe meant an almost complete reversal of previously held views. Today, we adhere to the heliocentric view as something already learned and believed during early school days. It is something that has become part of general knowledge and is simply taken for granted.

And yet, although we think that people in the Middle Ages and in more ancient times believed uniquely in the geocentric view as represented by Ptolemy, this was by no means always the case. We only need to read, for instance, what Plutarch wrote about the system of Aristarchus of Samos, who lived in ancient Greece in the prechristian era. Outer historical accounts mention Aristarchus' heliocentric view. Spiritual science makes the situation clear.

Aristarchus put the sun in the center of our planetary system, and let the earth circle around it. Indeed, if we take Aristarchus' heliocentric system in its main outlines—leaving aside further details supplied by more recent scientific research—we find it in full agreement with our present picture of the universe. What does this mean? Nothing more than that Aristarchus of Samos merely betrayed what was taught in the old mystery centers. Outside these schools, people were left to believe in what they could see with their own eyes. And why should this have been so? Why were ordinary people left with the picture of the universe as it appears to the eyes? Because the leaders of those schools believed that before anyone could be introduced to the heliocentric system, they had to cross an inner threshold into another world—a world entirely different from the one in which people ordinarily live. People were protected from that other world in their daily lives by the invisible Guardian of the Threshold, who was a very real, if supersensible, being to the ancient teachers. According to their view, human beings were to be protected from having their eyes suddenly opened to see a world that might appear bereft of soul and spirit.

But that is how we see the world today! We observe it and create our picture of the realms of nature—the mineral, plant, and animal kingdoms—only to find this picture soulless and spiritless. When we form a picture of the orbits and the movements of the heavenly bodies with the aid of calculations based on telescopic observations, we see a world empty of soul and spirit. The wise teachers of the mystery centers knew very well that it was possible to see the world in that way. But they transmitted such knowledge to their pupils only after the pupils had undergone the necessary preparations, after they had undergone a severe training of their will life. Then, they guided their pupils past the Guardian of the Threshold—but not until they were prepared. How was this preparation accomplished? Pupils had not only to endure great deprivations, but for many years they were also taught by their teachers to follow a moral path in strict obedience. At the same time, their will life was severely disciplined to strengthen their self-consciousness. And only after they had thus progressed from a dim self-consciousness to a more conscious one were they shown what lay ahead of them on the other side of the threshold: namely, the world as it appears to us in outer space according to the heliocentric system of the universe. At the same time, of course, they were also taught many other things that, to us, have merely become part of our general knowledge of the world.

Pupils in ancient times were thus carefully prepared before they were given the kind of knowledge that today is almost commonplace for every schoolboy and schoolgirl. This shows how times and whole civilizations have changed. Because external history knows nothing of the history of the development of the human soul, we tend to be under a misapprehension if we go only by what we read in history books.

What was it then, that pupils of the ancient mystery centers brought with them before crossing the threshold to the supersensible world? It was knowledge of the world that, to a certain extent, had arisen from their instinctual life, from the drives of their physical bodies. By means of those drives or instincts, they saw the external world ensouled and filled with spirit. That is now known as animism. They could feel how closely a human being was related to the outer world. They felt that their own spirit was embedded in the world spirit. At the same time, in order to look on the world as we learn to do already during our early school days, those ancient people had to undergo special preparations.

Nowadays, one can read all kinds of things about the Guardian of the Threshold—and the threshold to the spiritual world—in books whose authors take it upon themselves to deal with the subject of mysticism, often in dilettantish ways, even if their publications have an air of learnedness about them. Indeed, one often finds that, the more nebulous the mysticism, the greater attraction it seems to exert on certain sections of the public. But what I am talking about here, what is revealed to the unbiased spiritual investigator concerning what the ancients called the threshold to the spiritual world, is not the kind of nebulous mysticism that many sects and orders expound today and many people seek on the other side of the threshold. Rather, it is the kind of knowledge which has become a matter of general education today.

At the same time, we can see how we look at the world today with a very different self-consciousness than people did in more ancient times. The teachers of ancient wisdom were afraid that, unless their pupils' self-consciousness had been strengthened by a severe training of the will, they would suffer from overwhelming faintness of soul when they were told, for example, that the earth was not stationary but revolved around the sun with great speed, and that they too were circling around the sun. This feeling of losing firm ground from under their feet was something that the ancients would not have been able to bear. It would have reduced their self-consciousness to the level of a swoon. We, on the other hand, learn to stand up to it already in childhood.

We almost take for granted now the kind of world-view into which the people of ancient times were able to penetrate only after careful preparation. Yet we must not allow ourselves to have nostalgic feelings for ancient ways of living, which can no longer fulfill the present needs of the soul. Anthroposophical science of the spirit, of which I am speaking, is a renewal neither of ancient Eastern wisdom nor of old Gnostic teachings, for if such teachings were to be given today, they would have only a decadent effect. Spiritual science, on the other hand, is something to be found by an elementary creative power that lives in every human soul when certain paths that I will describe presently are followed. First, however, I want to draw attention to the fact that ordinary life, and science in general, already represents a kind of threshold to the supersensible world or, at any rate, to another world.

People living in ancient times had a quite different picture of life on the other side of the threshold. But what do we hear, especially from our most conscientious natural scientists, who feel thoroughly convinced of the rightness of their methods? We are told that natural science has reached the ultimate limits of knowledge. We hear such expressions as "*ignorabimus,*" "we shall never know," which—I hasten to add—is perfectly justified as long as we remain within the bounds of natural science.[4] Ancient peoples might have lacked our intense self-consciousness, but we are lacking in other ways.

To what do we owe our intense self-consciousness? We received it through the ways of thinking and looking at the world that entered our civilization with people like Copernicus, Galileo, Kepler, Bruno, and others.[5] The works of such thinkers not only provided us with a certain amount of knowledge but, through them, modern humanity underwent a distinct training of soul life. Everything that the mode of thinking developed by these personalities has achieved in more recent times tends to cultivate the powers of intellect. There is also a strong emphasis on scientific experimentation and on accurate, conscientious observation. With instruments such as the telescope, the microscope, X-rays, and the spectroscope, we examine the phenomena around us and we use our intellect mainly in order to extract from those phenomena their fundamental and inherent natural laws. But what are we actually doing when we are engaged in observing and experimenting? Our methods of working allow only the powers of reasoning and intellect to speak.

It is simply a fact that, during the last centuries, it has been primarily the intellect that has been tapped to promote human development. And a characteristic feature of the intellect is that it strengthens human self-consciousness, hardening it and making it more intense. Due to this hardening, we are able to bear what an ancient Greek could not have born; namely, the

---

4. The famous "ignorabimus" was first voiced by the German physiologist Emil Dubois-Reymond (1818–1896) in a lecture, *On the Limits of Natural Science*, given on August 14, 1872, in Leipzig. Steiner refers frequently to this moment. See, for instance, *The Riddles of Philosophy* or *The Boundaries of Natural Science.*

5. Nicolas Copernicus, 1473-1543; Galileo Galilei, 1564–1643; Johannes Kepler, 1571–1630; Giordano Bruno, 1548–1600.

consciousness of being moved around the sun on an earth that has no firm ground to uphold it. At the same time, because of this strengthened self-consciousness that has led to the picture of a world devoid of soul and spirit, we are deprived of the kind of knowledge for which our souls nevertheless yearn. We can see the world with its material phenomena—its material facts—as the ancients could never have seen it without appropriate preparation in the mystery centers, but we can no longer perceive a spiritual world surrounding us. This is why conscientious scientists confess "ignorabimus" and speak of limits to what we can know.

As human beings, we stand in the world. And, if we reflect on ourselves, we must inevitably realize that, whenever we ponder various things or draw conclusions based on experiment and observation, something spiritual is acting in us. And we must ask ourselves, "Is that spirit likely to live in isolation from the world of material phenomena like some kind of hermit? Does that spirit exist only in our physical bodies? Can it really be that the world is empty of soul and spirit, as the findings of the physical and biological sciences would have us believe and, from their point of view, quite rightly so?"

This is the situation in which we find ourselves at the present time. We are facing a new threshold. Although that circumstance has not yet penetrated the consciousness of humanity as a whole, awareness of it in human souls is not completely absent either. People might not be thinking about it but, in the depths of their souls, it lives nevertheless as a kind of presentiment. What goes on in the realm of the soul remains mostly unconscious. But out of that unconsciousness arises a longing to cross the threshold again, to add knowledge of the spiritual world to present self-consciousness.

No matter what name we might wish to give these things—that in most cases are felt only dimly—they nevertheless belong to the deepest riddles of our civilization. There is a sense that a spiritual world surrounding all human beings must be found again and that the soulless, spiritless world of which natural science speaks cannot be the one with which the human soul can feel inwardly united.

How can we rediscover the kind of knowledge that also generates a religious mood in us? That is the great question of our present time. How can we find a way of knowing that also, at the same time, fulfills our deepest need for an awareness of the eternal in the human soul? Modern science has achieved great and mighty things. Nevertheless, any unprejudiced person must acknowledge that it has not really produced solutions, but rather—one would almost have to say—the very opposite. Yet we should accept even this both willingly and gladly.

What can we do with the help of modern science? Does it help us to solve the riddles of the human soul? Hardly, but at least it prompts us to ask our questions at a deeper level. Contemporary science has put before us the material facts in all purity; that is, free from what a personal or subjective element might introduce in the form of soul and spirit. But, just because of this, we are made all the more intensely aware of the deep questions living in our souls. It is a significant achievement of contemporary science to have confronted us with new, ever deepening riddles. The great question of our time is therefore: what is our attitude toward these deepened riddles? What we can learn from the spirit of a Haeckel, Huxley, or Spencer does not make it possible to solve these riddles; it does, however, enable us to experience the great questions facing contemporary humanity more intensely than ever before.[6]

---

6. Ernst Haeckel (1834–1919); Thomas Huxley (1825–1895); Herbert Spencer (1820–1903). See Steiner, *The Riddles of Philosophy*, Part II.

This is where spiritual science—the science of the spirit—comes into its own, for its aim is to lead humanity, in a way that corresponds to its contemporary character, over the new threshold into a spiritual world. How this is possible for a modern person—as distinct from the man or woman of old—I should now like to indicate, if only in brief outline. You can find more detailed descriptions in my books *How to Know Higher Worlds* and *Occult Science*, and in other publications of mine.[7]

First, I would like to draw attention to the point of departure for anyone who wishes to engage in spiritual research or become a spiritual researcher. It is an inner attitude with which, due to present circumstances, a modern person is not likely to be in sympathy at all. It is an attitude of soul that I would like to call intellectual modesty or humility. Despite the fact that the intellect has developed to a degree unprecedented in human evolution during the past three or four hundred years, a would-be spiritual researcher must nevertheless achieve intellectual humility or modesty. Let me clarify what I mean by using a comparison. Imagine that you put a volume of Shakespeare's plays into the hands of a five-year-old. What would the child do? The child would play with the book, turn its pages, perhaps tear them. He or she would not use the book as it was meant to be used. But, ten-to-fifteen years later, that young person would have a totally different relationship to the same volume. He or she would treat the book according to its intended purpose. What has happened? Faculties that were dormant in the child have meanwhile developed through natural growth, upbringing, and education. During those ten to fifteen years, the child has become an altogether different soul being.

7. For instance, *Stages of Higher Knowledge* and *A Road to Self Knowledge and The Threshold of the Spiritual World.*

Now, an adult who has achieved intellectual humility, despite having absorbed the scientific climate of the environment by means of the intellect, might say: my relationship to the sense world may be compared with the relationship of a five-year-old child to a volume of Shakespeare's plays. Faculties that are capable of further development might lie dormant within me. I too could grow into an altogether different being as far as my soul and spirit are concerned and understand the sense world more deeply.

Nowadays, however, people do not like to adopt an attitude of such intellectual modesty. Habits of thought and the psychological response to life as it is steer us in a different direction. Those who have gone through the usual channels of education might enter higher education, where it is no longer a question of deepening inner knowledge and of developing faculties of will and soul. For, during a scientific training of that kind, a person remains essentially at the level of his or her inherited capacities and what ordinary education can provide. Certainly, science has expanded tremendously by means of experimentation and observation, but that expansion has only been achieved by means of those intellectual powers that already exist in what is usually called modern culture. In furthering knowledge, the aim of science has not been to cultivate new faculties in the human being. The thought would never have occurred that anyone already in possession of our present means of knowledge, as given both by ordinary life and by science, might actually be confronting the world of nature in a way similar to how a five-year old responds to a volume of Shakespeare. Allowance has not been made for the possibility that new faculties of cognition could develop that would substantially alter our attitude toward the external world. That such new faculties are possible, however, is precisely the attitude required of anyone who wishes to investigate the spiritual world of which anthroposophy, the science of the spirit, speaks. Here, the aim is to develop human faculties inherent in each person. However, in order to bring these potentials to a certain stage of development, a great deal must be experienced first.

I am not talking about taking extraordinary or even superstitious measures for the sake of this soul development. Rather, I am talking about the enhancement of quite ordinary, well known faculties that play important roles both in daily life and in the established sciences. However, although those faculties are being applied all the time, they are not developed to their full extent during the life between birth and death.

There are many such faculties, but I would like to characterize today the further development of only two of them. More detailed information can be found in the books mentioned previously.

First of all, there is the faculty of remembering or memory, which is an absolute necessity in life. It is generally realized—as anyone with a particular interest in these matters will know from books on psychology and pathology—how important it is for a healthy soul life that a person's memory should be unimpaired and that our memory should allow us to look back over our past life right down to early childhood. There must not exist periods in our past from which memory pictures cannot rise to bring events back again. If someone's memory were to be completely erased, the ego or I of such a person would be virtually destroyed. Severe soul sickness would befall such an individual. Memory gives us the possibility for past experiences to resurface, whether in pale or in vivid pictures. It is this faculty, this force, that can be strengthened and developed further. What is its characteristic quality? Without it, experiences flit by without leaving any lasting trace. Also, without memory, the concepts formed through such experiences would be only fleeting ones. Our memory stores up such experiences for us (here,

I can give only sketchy indications; in my writings and published lectures you will find a scientifically built-up treatment of memory).[8]

Memory gives duration to otherwise fleeting impressions. This quality of memory is grasped as a first step in applying spiritual-scientific methods. It is then intensified and developed further through what I have called meditation and concentration in the books that I have mentioned. To practice these two activities, a student, having sought advice from someone experienced in these matters or having gained the necessary information from appropriate literature, will focus consciousness on certain interrelated mental images that are clearly defined and easy to survey. They could be geometrical or mathematical patterns that one can clearly view and that one is certain are not reminiscences from life, emerging from one's subconscious.

Whatever is held in consciousness in this way must result from a person's free volition. One must in no way allow oneself to become subject to auto suggestion or dreaming. One contemplates what one has chosen to place in the center of one's consciousness and holds it for a longer period of time in complete inner tranquility. Just as muscles develop when engaged in a particular type of work, so certain soul forces unfold when the soul is engaged in the uncustomary activity of arresting and holding definite mental images. It sounds simple enough. But, in fact, not only are there people who believe that, when speaking about these things, a scientist of the spirit is drawing on obscure influences, but there are others who believe it simple to achieve the methods that I am describing here, methods that are applied in intimate regions of one's soul life.

---

8. See, for instance, *Anthroposophy and the Inner Life.*

Far from it! These things take a long time to accomplish. Of course, some find it easier to practice these exercises, but others have to struggle much harder. Naturally, the depth of such meditation is far more important than the length of time spent over it. Whatever the case might be, however, one must persevere in one's efforts for years. What one practices in one's soul in this way is truly no easier than what one does in a laboratory, in a lecture hall for physics, or an astronomical observatory. It is in no way more difficult to fulfill the demands imposed by external forms of research than it is to practice faithfully, carefully, and conscientiously what spiritual research requires to be cultivated in the human soul over a period of many years.

Nevertheless, as a consequence of such practice, certain inner soul forces, previously known to us only as forces of memory, eventually gain in strength and new soul powers come into existence. Such inner development enables one to recognize clearly what the materialistic interpretation is saying about the power of memory when it maintains that the human faculty of remembering is bound to the physical body and that, if there is something wrong with the constitution of the nervous system, memory is weakened, as it is likewise in old age. Altogether, spiritual faculties are seen to depend on physical conditions. As far as life between birth and death is concerned, this is not denied by spiritual science. For whoever develops the power of memory as I have described knows through direct insight how ordinary memory, which conjures up pictures of past experiences before the soul, does indeed depend on the human physical body. On the other hand, the new soul forces now being developed become entirely *free and independent of the physical body.* The student thereby experiences how it becomes possible to live in a region of the soul in such a way that one can have supersensible experiences, just as one has sense-perceptible experiences in the physical body.

I would now like to give you an explanation of the nature of these supersensible experiences.

Human life undergoes rhythmical changes between waking and sleeping. The moments of falling asleep and awakening, and the time spent in sleep, are interspersed with waking life. What happens in this process? When we fall asleep, our consciousness is dimmed down, in most cases to a zero point. Dreams sometimes "bubble up" from halfconscious depths. Obviously, we are alive during this condition for, otherwise, as sleepers, we would have to pass away every night and come to life again every morning. The human soul and spirit are alive but, during sleep, our consciousness is diminished. This diminution of consciousness has to do with our inability to employ our senses between when we fall asleep and when we wake up, and also with our lack of access to impulses that derive from our physical organs of will.

This dimming down of consciousness can be overcome by those who have developed the new higher faculty of which I have spoken of their given faculty of memory. Such people reach a condition, as they do in sleep, in which they no longer need eyes in order to see, nor ears in order to hear. They no longer need to feel the physical warmth of their environment, nor to use will impulses that under ordinary conditions work through the muscles and through the human physical organization generally. They are able to switch off everything connected with the physical body. And yet their consciousness does not diminish as is usually the case in sleep. On the contrary, they are able to surrender themselves in full consciousness to conditions normally pertaining only to the sleeping state. A spiritual researcher remains completely conscious. Just as a sleeping person is surrounded by a dark world of nothingness, so a spiritual researcher is surrounded by a world that has nothing to do with the sense world but is nevertheless as full and intense as the sense world. In the waking state, we confront the sense world with our senses. But when they are able to free themselves from the physical body in full consciousness—that is, when they can enter, fully consciously, the state normally gone through between falling asleep and waking up—spiritual researchers confront a supersensible world.

They thus learn to recognize that a supersensible world always surrounds us, just as the sense world surrounds us in ordinary life. Yet there is a significant difference. In the sense world, we perceive outer facts through our senses and, through those facts, we also become aware of the existence of other beings. Outer *facts* predominate while beings or existences make their presence felt within the context of these outer facts. But, when the supersensible world is opened to us, we first encounter *beings*.[9] As soon as our eyes are opened to behold the supersensible world, real beings surround us. To begin with, we cannot call this world of concrete and real supersensible beings in which we now find ourselves a world of facts. We must gain such facts for ourselves by means of yet something else.It is an achievement of the modern anthroposophical science of the spirit that it enables human beings to cross a threshold once more and enter a world different from what usually surrounds us.

After one has learned to experience the state of independence from the physical body, one finally comes to realize not only that the soul during sleep lifts itself out of the body only to return to it upon awakening, but also that this return is caused by the soul's intense desire for the physical body. Supersensible cognition enables us to recognize the true nature of the soul, whose re-entry into the physical body upon awakening is due to a craving for the body as it lies asleep. Furthermore, if

---

9. See, for instance, Rudolf Steiner, *Spiritual Beings in the Heavenly Bodies and in the Kingdoms of Nature.*

one can make this true conception of falling asleep and awakening one's own, one's understanding expands to such an extent that one eventually learns to know the soul before it descends—through conception and birth—from the spiritual world into the physical body offered by heredity.

Once one has grasped the nature of the human soul, and has learned to follow it outside the body between falling asleep and waking up—at the same time recognizing the less powerful forces pulling it back into the body lying in the bed—then one also begins to know what happens to the soul when it is freed from the body and passes through the portal of death. One learns to understand that the reason why the human soul has only a dim consciousness during sleep is because it has a strong desire to return to the body. It is this craving for the body that can dull human consciousness into a state of total impotence during the time between falling asleep and awakening. On the other hand, once the soul has passed through death, this desire for the physical body is no longer there.

And once, through the newly developed faculty of enhanced memory, we have learned to know the human soul, we can follow its further progress beyond the portal of death.[10] One then learns to recognize that, since it is no longer bound to a physical body and is therefore freed from the desire to return to it, the soul is now in a position to retain a consciousness of its own while in the spiritual world, a consciousness that differs from what is given through the instrument of the physical body. One comes to recognize that there were forces in the soul before birth that drew it toward a physical body while it was still in the spiritual world. That physical body, however, was as yet quite indeterminate; it cast a certain light toward the descending soul. Then one begins to see how the soul develops

10. See Rudolf Steiner, *The Presence of the Dead.*

a strong desire to re-enter physical, earthly life. One learns to know—but in a different language—the eternal being of the human soul. This being becomes clear and, through it, one learns to understand something else as well.

One learns to cognize in pictures the soul's eternal being as it goes through births and deaths. I have called those pictures *imaginations.*[11] And one comes to recognize that, just as the body belongs to the sensory world, so too does the soul belong to a supersensible world; and that, just as one can describe the sense world with the help of the physical body, so can one likewise describe the supersensible world with its spirituality. One comes to know the supersensible world in addition to the sensory world. But, in order to attain this faculty, it is necessary to cultivate another soul quality, the mere mention of which—as a way of gaining higher knowledge—is enough to make a modern scientist wince. Certainly, one can fully respect the reasons for this, but what I have to tell you about the enhancement of this second soul faculty is nevertheless true.

As I said, the first power to be developed is the faculty of memory, which then becomes an independent force. The second power to be developed is the power of *love.* In ordinary life, between birth and death, love works through the physical organism. It is intimately connected with the instincts and drives of human nature and only in sublime moments does something of this love free itself from human corporeality. In those moments, we experience being freed from our narrow selves. Such love is a state of true freedom, in which one does not surrender to inborn instincts, but rather forgets the ordinary self and orients one's actions and deeds toward outer needs and facts. It was because of this intimate connection between love and freedom that I dared to state publicly in my

11. See Rudolf Steiner, *Life between Death and Rebirth.*

book, *Intuitive Thinking as a Spiritual Path*[12] (first published in 1892 and in which I tried to found a new sociology in philosophical terms), that, far from making people blind, love makes them see; that is, free. Love leads us beyond what otherwise blinds us by making us dependent on personal needs. Love allows us to surrender to the outer world. It removes whatever would hinder our acting in full freedom. The modern spiritual investigator must therefore develop such love—love that shines actively into ordinary life in truly free deeds. Gradually, love must be spiritualized, in the same way as the faculty of remembering had to be spiritualized. Love must become purely a power of the soul. It must make the human individual as a soul being entirely independent of the body, so that he or she can love free from blood ties and from the physical organization as a whole. Love of this kind brings about a fusion of the self with the external world, with one's fellow human beings. Through love, one becomes one with the world.

This newly developed power of love has another consequence. It makes us "co-workers" in the spiritual world that we have been able to enter through the newly developed faculty of memory. At this point, we learn to know real beings as spiritual facts. When describing the external world, we now no longer speak of our present planetary system as having originated from some primeval cosmic nebula and of its falling into dust again—or into the sun again—in some remote future. We do not contemplate nature as being thus alienated from the world of spirit. And, if people today are honest, they cannot help becoming aware of the dichotomy between what is most precious in them on one hand, and the interpretation of the world given by natural science on the other. How often has one come

12. Also translated as *The Philosophy of Spiritual Activity* or *The Philosophy of Freedom.*

across oppressed souls saying, "Natural science speaks of a world of pure necessity. It tells us that the world originated from a primeval mist. This condensed into the natural kingdoms—the mineral, plant and animal kingdoms and, finally, also the human kingdom. And yet, deep inside us, something rises that surely is of fundamental importance and value, namely, our moral and religious world. This stands before our souls as the one thing that makes us truly human. But an honest interpretation of the world of natural science tells us that this earth, on which we stand with our moral ideas like hermits in the universe, will disintegrate, will fall back again into the sun, it will end up as one vast cinder. A large cemetery is all that will be left and all of our ideals will be buried there."

This is the point at which spiritual science enters, not just to grant new hope and belief, but resting entirely on its own sure knowledge, developed as I have already described. It states that the natural-scientific theory of the world offers only an abstract point of view. In reality, the world is imbued with spirit, and permeated by supersensible beings. If we look back into primeval times, we find that the material substances of the earth originated in the spiritual world, and also that the present material nature of the earth will become spirit again in future times. Just as, at death, the human being lays aside the physical body to enter, consciously, a spiritual world, so will the material part of the earth fall away like a corpse and what then is soul and spirit on earth and in human beings will arise again in future times, even though the earth will have perished. Christ's words—taken as a variation of this same theme—ring true: "Heaven and earth shall pass away, but my words shall not pass away."[13] Human beings thus can say, "Everything that our eyes can see will perish, just as the body, the transient part of the human

13. St. Luke 21:33.

individuality, does. But there will rise again from this dying away what lived on earth as morality. Human beings will perceive a spiritual world around them; they will live themselves into a spiritual world."

In this way, deepening knowledge with spirit, anthroposophical spiritual science meets the needs of our present civilization differently from external science. It deepens knowledge and cognition to the level of deeply felt piety, of religious consciousness, giving human beings spiritual self-awareness.

Fundamentally speaking, this is the great question faced by contemporary civilization. But, as long as human beings lack the proper inner stability, as long as they feel themselves to be material entities floating about in some vacuum, they cannot develop a strong inner being, nor play a vigorous part in social life. Outer planning and organization, directly affecting social conditions, must be created by people themselves. Such outer social conditions are of great significance to the questions of present and future civilization—questions that lead us to search for true consciousness of our humanity. But only those with inner stability, which has been granted them through being anchored in the spirit, will be able to take their proper place in social life.

Thus, a first question is, how can people place themselves into present social conditions with inner firmness and certainty regarding matters of daily life? A second question concerns human relationships or what we could call our attitude toward our fellow human beings: the way in which each person meets his or her fellow human being. Here we enter a realm where, no less than in the realm of knowledge, modern civilization has brought us new riddles rather than new solutions. Only think of how the achievements of modern natural science have expanded the scope of technology! The technology, commerce, and transportation that surround us every hour of the day are all offspring of this new, grandiose way of looking at the sense-perceptible world. And yet we have not been able to find an answer in this age of technology to what has become a new, vital question; namely, how are we, as human beings, to live in this complex technical, commercial and traffic-ridden world? This question has become a by-product of modern civilization itself. The fact that it has not yet been resolved can be seen in the devastating political movements, the destructiveness of which increases the farther east we go, even right into Asia.[14] Due to a working out of human instincts, nothing noble or elevating is being put into the world there. Rather, because the burning questions of our day have not been solved, havoc and destruction rule the day. There is no doubt that modern civilization would perish if what is emerging in the East were to spread worldwide. What is lurking there, intent on bringing about the downfall of modern civilization, is far more horrific than people living in the West can imagine. But it also testifies to the fact that something else is needed for the solution of the problem of contemporary civilization.

It is not enough for us to work within the bounds of modern technology, which is a child of the modern world outlook. We must also work toward attainment of another possibility. Human beings have become estranged from their old kinship to nature. In their practical activities and in their professional lives, they have been placed into a soulless, spiritually empty, mechanistic world. From cooperating with nature, they have been led to operating machines and to dealing with spiritless and mechanical means of transportation. We must find the way again to give them something to take the place of the old kinship to nature. And this can only be a world-view that speaks to our souls with a powerful voice, making us realize

14. Steiner is referring to the Bolshevik Revolution.

that there is more to human life than what can be experienced outwardly. Human beings must become inwardly certain that they belong to a supersensible world, to a world of soul and spirit, that always surrounds them. They must see that it is possible to investigate that world with the same scientific accuracy as the physical world, which is being studied and explored by outer science and which has led to this technological age. Only such a new science of the supersensible can become the foundation for a new, right relationship between people. Such a science not only will allow them to see in their fellow human beings what appears during the life between birth and death, but will make them recognize and respect what is immortal and eternal in human beings through their humanity's close links with a spiritual world. Such a deepened knowledge will surely bring about a change for the better in how one individual perceives another.

Here is yet a third point of importance. It is the recognition that human life is not fully exhausted within the boundaries of birth and death, as the "ideology of the proletariat" would have us believe. Rather, what we are doing every moment here on earth is of significance not only for the earth, but for the whole of the universe. When the earth will have passed away, what we have carried into our daily tasks out of moral, soul-and-spiritual depths will arise to live in another world. Transformed, it will become part of a general spiritualization.[15]

Thus anthroposophical spiritual science approaches the problems of our time in a threefold way. It enables us to become aware of our spirituality. It helps us see in our fellows other beings of soul and spirit. And it helps us recognize that our earthly deeds, however humble and practical, have a cosmic and universal spiritual meaning.

---

15. See Rudolf Steiner, *The Apocalypse of St. John.*

In working towards these aims, spiritual science has been active not only in theory; it has also entered the sphere of practical life. In Stuttgart, there is the Waldorf school, which was founded by Emil Molt and which I was asked to direct.[16] It is a school whose pedagogical principles and methods are based on insights gained through the science of the spirit I am speaking of here. Furthermore, in Dornach, near Basel, lies the Goetheanum, which houses our High School of Spiritual Science. This Goetheanum in Dornach is still incomplete, but we were already able to hold a large number of courses in the unfinished building during the autumn of last year.[17]

Some time ago, on a previous occasion, I was also asked to speak about spiritual science here in Holland. At that time, I could say only that it existed as a new method of research and that it was something inherently alive in every human being. Since then, spiritual science has taken on a different form. It has begun to establish its own High School in Dornach. Last spring, I was able to show how what I could only sketch tonight as the beginning of spiritual-scientific research can be applied in all branches of science. On that occasion, I showed doctors and medical students how the results of spiritual science, gained by means of strict and exact methods, can be applied to therapeutics.[18] Medical questions, which can often

---

16. Emil Molt, 1876–1936, manager of the Waldorf-Astoria cigarette factory in Stuttgart. Inspired by the movement for the Threefold Social Order, Molt founded the Waldorf School in Stuttgart, initially only for the children of the workers employed in his factory. At Molt's request, Rudolf Steiner took over the general planning and leadership of the school.
17. For the lectures, see Rudolf Steiner, *The Boundaries of Natural Science.* Regarding the Goetheanum itself, see Rex Raab, Arne Klingborg, and Åke Fant, *Eloquent Concrete* (London: Rudolf Steiner Press, 1979). For the High School of Spiritual Science, see *The Constitution of the School of Spiritual Science* (London: Anthroposophical Society in Great Britain, 1964).
18. See Rudolf Steiner, *Spiritual Science and Medicine.*

touch on other problems related to general human health, are questions that every conscientious doctor recognizes as belonging to the facts of our present civilization. They have become riddles because modern science will not rise from observing only what is sense perceptible and widen its investigations to include the supersensible, the spiritual world. During that autumn course, specialists drawn from many fields—including law, mathematics, history, sociology, biology, physics, chemistry, and pedagogy—tried to show how all branches of science can be fructified by anthroposophical spiritual science. Representatives of the arts were also present to demonstrate how spiritual science was inspiring them to discover new developments in their professions. Then there were others, too, drawn from such spheres of practical life as commerce and industry. These could show that spiritual science not only lifted them out of the old routines that led the world into the catastrophe of the last war, but also that it can help relate people to practical life in a higher sense. The courses were meant to show how spiritual science, far from fostering dilettantism or nebulous mysticism, is capable of entering and fructifying all of the sciences and that, in doing so, it is uplifting and linking each separate branch to become a part of a comprehensive spiritual-supersensible conception of the human being.

I shall have more to say next time about the practical applications of spiritual science, particularly with regard to education and the social question. Once I have done so, you will appreciate that anthroposophical spiritual science is not striving for some vague mysticism, removed from daily life, but wishes to grasp the spirit consciously. It wishes to do so for two main reasons—first, because it is essential for human beings to become aware of how they are related to their true spiritual origin and, second, because spiritual powers are intent on intervening in the practical and material affairs of daily life.

Anyone, therefore, who tends to combine a life devoid of spirit with a truly practical life, or combine a spiritual attitude with isolation from daily life, has certainly not grasped the real nature of anthroposophical spiritual science, nor recognized the paramount needs of our present age.

We have found people who understand what the High School of Spiritual Science seeks to accomplish for the benefit of humanity along the lines already indicated. We have found people who appreciate the necessity of working in this way in view of the great problems facing our present civilization. Yet, due to difficult local circumstances, the completion of the Goetheanum has been greatly delayed. This building is still in an unfinished state and its completion will largely depend on continued help from friends who have the heart and the understanding to give their support for the sake of human evolution, so needed today. Nevertheless, despite these difficulties, more than a thousand people were assembled at the opening of our courses. Visitors can see in Dornach that spiritual science seeks to work out of the whole human being, that it does not wish to appeal only to the head. They can witness that it seeks to move ahead not only through what can be gained by experimentation and observation, but also by striving for truly artistic expression, free from empty symbolism or pedantic allegory. This is the reason why we could not possibly use just any arbitrary style for our building in Dornach. Its architecture, too, had to flow from the same sources from which spiritual science itself flows. Because it endeavors to draw on the whole human being, spiritual science is less one-sided than the other sciences, which work only on the basis of experimentation and observation. It is as exact as any other science could be and, in addition, wants to speak to the whole human being.

About the practical aspects, I shall have more to say next time. Today, I wanted to prepare the ground by showing how spiritual research leads us right into our present situation. When dealing with the practical side, I hope to show how our times are in need of what anthroposophical spiritual science has to offer. Such spiritual science seeks to complement the conscientious and methodical research into the world of matter, which it acknowledges more than any other spiritual movement. It is also capable of leading to a religious deepening and to artistic impulses, as did the old, instinctive science of the mystery centers, renewal of which, however, would no longer serve our present needs.

When dealing with the practical aspects, I shall have to show that spiritual science is in no way either antireligious or anti-Christian. Like all other true and religious aspirations toward an inner deepening, spiritual science strives toward the spirit.

This gives us the hope that those who still oppose spiritual science will eventually find their way into it because it strives toward something belonging to all people. It strives toward the spirit, and humanity needs the spirit.

2

Education and Practical Life from the Perspective of Spiritual Science

THE HAGUE — FEBRUARY 27, 1921

In my first lecture, I drew your attention to the essence of anthroposophical spiritual science. I mentioned how methods have been sought in spiritual science that enable the spiritual investigator to penetrate a supersensible world with the same clarity as natural science penetrates the outer, sense-perceptible world with the sense organs and the intellect, which systematizes and interprets the results of sensory impressions. I described these methods in my last lecture. And I emphasized that, in addition to today's ordinary science, another science exists. This uses spiritual methods and, by its path of research and the inner experiences unfolding along it, furnishes full proof of our being surrounded by a supersensible world, just as, in the ordinary state of consciousness, we are surrounded by the sense world. I would now like to return to a prior point, elaborated during the last lecture, that, at least to a certain extent, will form the basis of what I have to say today.

The anthroposophical science of the spirit, referred to here, is not at all opposed to what has become—over the last three or four centuries—the natural-scientific world-view. As I already pointed out, this spiritual science is opposed only to viewpoints that do not take into account the results of modern natural science and thereby become more or less dilettantish. Spiritual science wishes to be an extension or continuation of natural-scientific thinking. Only, this spiritual-scientific continuation allows a person to acquire the kind of knowledge that can answer the deepest longings in the minds and the souls of modern human beings. Thus, through spiritual science, one really comes to know human beings.

Not so long ago, modern science, in a way fully recognized by spiritual science, gave us a wonderful survey of the gradual development of living organisms right up to human beings. And yet, when all is said and done, the human being stands there *only* as the end product of evolution.

Biology speaks of certain muscles that are found both in human beings and in various animal species. We also know that a human being has a certain number of bones and that this number corresponds with the bones of the higher animals. Altogether, we have grown accustomed to explaining the emergence of the entire bone structure of higher animals and human beings as a development from a lower stage to a higher one. But we have no idea of the essential characteristics that are uniquely and exclusively human. Anyone willing to look at the situation without prejudice has to admit the fact that we are ignorant of what constitutes a human being. In general, natural phenomena and all living organisms are scrupulously investigated up to and including *homo sapiens*, and the conclusion is then drawn that human beings are encompassed by what is to be found in external nature. But, generally, there is no really adequate idea of what is essentially human.

In ordinary, practical life, we find a similar situation, very much as a result of natural-scientific thinking and knowledge. We find its effects overshadowing modern life, causing a great deal of perplexity and distress. The consequence of not knowing the essential nature of human beings becomes all too obvious in what is usually referred to as the social question. Millions of people who belong to what is called the proletariat, whom the traditional religions and confessions have abandoned, believe that reality is no longer to be found in the human soul, but only in the material aspects of life, in the processes of production within the outer economic sphere. Morality, religion, science, and art, as cultivated by humanity throughout the ages, are regarded as nothing more than a kind of ideological superstructure, built on a solid material or even economic material substructure. The moral and cultural aspects of life appear almost as a kind of vapor, rising from the only reality—material reality. Here, again, what is truly the human soul and spirit—what is psychical-spiritual in human beings—has been eliminated.[1]

Not to be able to reach knowledge of the human being and, consequently, to be debarred from beholding and experiencing the truth of human nature, and from bringing down human ideals into will impulses in the social sphere—these seem to be the characteristic features of modern times.

Anthroposophical spiritual science, on the other hand, is only too aware of what needs to be accomplished in this direction for the sake of the deepest, yet often unconscious, longing of the souls of some of the best of our contemporaries. It is to be accomplished, first, by true knowledge of the human being and, second, by an inner sense of fulfillment strong enough to enable one to carry into public life truly social impulses arising in the soul. For, without these impulses arising from the depths of our humanity, even the best of outer practical arrangements will not lead to what in the widest circles is regarded as unrealizable, but toward which many people are striving nevertheless, namely to a dignified human existence.

---

1. Steiner is referring to Marxism. See his essay "Marxism and the Threefold Social Order" in *The Renewal of the Social Organism*.

The path leading into the spiritual world as I described it here a few days ago could easily be understood as something that estranges one from life rather than leading one to the two weighty questions that I have put before you once again today. For this reason, it was of paramount importance that anthroposophical spiritual science be *practiced* in the Goetheanum in Dornach, Switzerland. Despite the unfinished state of the building, spiritual science has the possibility of pursuing practical activities there, demonstrating how knowledge of human nature and human faculties can enter into the practical sphere of life.

One of the most important practical activities is surely education of the young.

Those who work in the field of educating children are basically dealing with what will enter the world with the next generation, and this means a very great deal. Raising and educating children are a direct way to work into the near future. In its quest for a method of understanding human nature, anthroposophical spiritual science finds itself able to understand the human being in its becoming—the child—in a wide, comprehensive manner. From such comprehensive knowledge of the growing child, spiritual science seeks to create a real art of education. For what spiritual science can provide in understanding and penetration of human nature does not end in abstractions or theories, but eventually develops into an artistic comprehension, first of the human form and then of the potential of the human soul and spirit. It is all very well to maintain that science demands what is often called a sober working with objective concepts. But, ladies and gentlemen, what if the whole world, if nature, did not work with such concepts at all? What if it were to scorn our wish to restrict its creativity to the kind of natural law into which we try to confine it? What if the creativity of the world were to elude our sober, merely external grasp and our rather lightweight logical concepts? We can certainly make our demands, but whether by doing so we will attain real knowledge depends on whether nature works and creates according to them.

At any rate, more recent scientific attitudes have failed to recognize the essence of human nature because they have failed to consider the following. In her upward climb, at each successive step of the evolutionary ladder—from the mineral kingdom, through the plant and animal kingdoms, to the human kingdom—nature's creativity increasingly escapes our intellectual grasp and sober logic, forcing us to approach her workings more and more artistically. What ultimately lives in a human being is open to many interpretations and shows manifold aspects. And because spiritual science, in its own way, seeks the inner harmony between knowledge, religious depth, and artistic creativity, it is in a position to survey rightly—that is, spiritually—the enigmatic, admirable creation that is a human being and how it is placed in the world.

Last time, I spoke of how it is possible to look with scientific accuracy into the world where human beings live before they descend into physical existence at conception or birth. I indicated how, with mathematical clarity, the human spirit and soul, descending from the spiritual worlds, place themselves before the spiritual eyes of the anthroposophical investigator, showing themselves to be at work on the interior of the future earthly body and drawing only material substances from the stream of heredity bequeathed by previous generations.

Anyone who talks about such things today is quickly judged inconsistent. And yet the methods pursued by spiritual science are much the same as those employed by natural science. The main difference is that the work entailed in the various branches of natural science is done in the appropriate laboratories, clinics, or astronomical observatories, whereas the science of the spirit approaches human nature directly in order to observe it as methodically as a natural scientist observes whatever might belong to his or her particular field of study. In the latter case, however, the situation is more straightforward for it is easier to make one's observations and to search for underlying laws in natural science than in spiritual science.

As a first step, I would like to draw your attention to what one can observe in a growing human being in a truly natural-scientific way. Of course, in the case of spiritual science, we must include in our observations the gradual development of the human being through several different life periods. One of those periods extends from birth to the change of the teeth; that is, until about the seventh year. To recognize a kind of nodal point around the seventh year might easily create the impression of an inclination toward mysticism which is not, however, the case. The following observations have as little to do with mysticism as the distinction between the seven colors of the rainbow has. They are simply an outcome of objective, scientific observation of the growing child. Even from a physical point of view, it is evident that a powerful change occurs when, in about a child's seventh year, forces from within drive the second teeth out of the organism. This event does not recur, indicating that some kind of conclusion has been reached.

What is going on becomes clearer when we do not restrict our observations to the physical or change-of-teeth aspect of this seventh year, but extend them to parallel developments occurring alongside the physical changes. In this case, if we are capable of observing at all, we will see how a child's entire soul life undergoes a gradual change during this period. We can observe how the child, who previously could form only blurred and indistinct concepts, now begins to form more sharply contoured concepts—how it is only now in fact that the child begins to form proper concepts at all. Furthermore, we notice how quite a different kind of memory is now unfolding. Formerly, when younger, the child might often have displayed signs of an excellent memory. That memory, however, was entirely natural and instinctive. Whereas there was before no need for any special effort in the act of remembering, the child who has passed this watershed must now make a mental effort to remember past events clearly. In short, it becomes obvious that, with the change of teeth around the seventh year, a child begins to be active in the realm of mental imagery, in forming simple thoughts, and in the sphere of conscious will activity.

But what is actually happening here? Where had this force been that we can now observe in the child's soul and spirit, forming more clearly-defined mental images and thoughts? Where was that force before the child's milk teeth were shed? This is the kind of question that remains unasked by our contemporary theorizing psychologists.

When physicists observe in a physical process an increase of warmth that is not due to external causes, they explain this phenomenon by the concept of "latent heat becoming liberated." This implies that the heat that emerges must have existed previously within the substance itself. A similar kind of thinking must also be applied in the case of human life. Where were those forces of soul and spirit before they emerged in the child after the seventh year? They were latent in the child's physical organism. They were active in its organic growth, in its organic structuring, until, with the pushing out of the second teeth, a kind of climax was reached, indicating the conclusion of this first period of growth, so particularly active during the child's early years.

Psychology today is quite abstract. People cogitate on the relationship of soul to body, and devise the most remarkable and grandiloquent hypotheses. Empty phrases, however, will not lead to an art of education. Spiritual science, for its part, shows that what we see emerging cognitively in a child after the seventh year was actively engaged in its inner organism before the second dentition. It shows that what appears in a child's soul after the change of teeth was active before as an organic force that has now become liberated.

In a similar way, a true spiritual researcher observes in a concrete manner—not abstractly—the entire course of human life. To illustrate that concrete manner of observation, let us now consider a well-known and specific childhood phenomenon.

Let us look at children at play, at children's games. If we can do so without preconception and with dedicated interest in the growing human being, we know—although every game has a certain form and shares common, characteristic features—that, whatever the game, each child will play it with his or her own individual style. Now those who raise or educate young children can, to a certain extent, influence or guide how a child plays according to the child's own nature. Also, depending on our pedagogical skills, we can try to steer our children's play into more purposeful directions. And, if we pay attention to all this, we can clearly discriminate between the various individual styles of playing until the child reaches an age when they are no longer so clearly identifiable. Once a child enters school and other interests are crowding in, however, it becomes more difficult to see the future consequences of his or her characteristic style of playing. Nevertheless, if we do not observe superficially and, realizing that the course of life represents a whole, extend the range of our observations to span the entire earthly life, we might discover the following.

Around twenty-four or twenty-five—that is, when young adults must find their links with the outer world, and when they must fit themselves into the social fabric of the wider community—there will be those who prove themselves more skillful than others in dealing with all aspects and details of their tasks. Now, careful observation will reveal that the way in which people in their twenties adapt themselves to outer conditions of life, with greater or lesser skill, is a direct consequence of their play activity during early childhood.

Certain rivers, whose sources may be clearly traced, disappear below the earth's surface during their course, only to resurface at a later stage. We can compare this phenomenon with certain faculties in human life. The faculty of playing, so prominent in a young child, is particularly well developed during the first years of life. It then vanishes into the deeper regions of the soul to resurface during the twenties, transmuted into an aptitude for finding one's way in the world. Just think: by guiding the play of young children, we, as educators, are directly intervening in the happiness or unhappiness, the future destiny, of young people in their twenties!

Such insights greatly sharpen our sense of responsibility as educators. They also stimulate the desire to work toward a genuine art of education. Tight-fitting, narrow concepts cannot reach the core of human nature. To do so, a wide and comprehensive view is needed. Such a view can be gained if we recognize that such interconnections as I have mentioned affect human life. It will also make us realize that we must distinguish between definite life periods in human development, the first of which extends from birth to the change of teeth and has a character all its own.

At this point, I should mention that those who choose to become teachers or educators through anthroposophical spiritual science are filled with the consciousness that a message from the spiritual world is actually present in what they meet in such enigmatic and wondrous ways in the developing human being, the child. Such teachers observe the child with its initially indeterminate features, noticing how they gradually assume more definite forms. They see how children's movements and life stirrings are undefined to begin with and how directness and purpose then increasingly enter their actions from the depths of their souls. Those who have prepared themselves to become teachers and educators through anthroposophical spiritual science are aware that something actually descending from the spiritual worlds lives in the way the features of a child's face change from day to day, week to week, and year to year, gradually evolving into a distinct physiognomy. And they know too that something spiritual is descending in what is working through the lively movements of a child's hands and in what, quite magically, enters into a child's way of speaking.

To learn to recognize this activity of the spiritual world, which is so different from that of the physical world; to meet the child as an educator with such an inner attitude and mood as I have described: this means that we see in the vocation of teaching a source of healing. This vocation could be expressed as follows: *The spiritual worlds have entrusted a human soul into my care. I have been called upon to assist in solving the riddles that this child poses. By means of a deepened knowledge of the human being—transformed into a real art, the art of education—it is my task to show this child the way into life.*

Such deepened knowledge of human nature reveals that, in the first period of life, a child is what I would like to call an "imitating" being. (You will find a more detailed account of this characteristic feature in my booklet *The Education of the Child in the Light of Anthroposophy.*[2]) Descending from the spiritual world, the child brings to outer expression—like an echo from the spiritual world—the last experiences undergone there. As anthroposophists, when we educate our children, we are aware that the way in which children imitate their surroundings is childish and primitive. They copy what is done before them with their movements. They learn to speak entirely and only through imitation. And, until they lose their

2. See Bibliography.

milk teeth, they also imitate what happens morally in their environment.

What lies behind all of this can be rightly understood only with the help of spiritual science. Before conception or birth, a child lives in the spiritual world, the same spiritual world that can be known and consciously experienced if we strengthen the power of memory and develop the power of love in the ways I described during our last meeting. In that spiritual world, the relationship of one being to another is not one in which they confront one another outwardly; rather, each being is capable of living right into another—objectively, yet full of love. Children then bring this relationship of spiritual beings to one another down to earth. It is like a resonant echo of the spiritual world. We can observe here how children become creatures of imitation, how everything they learn and make their own during these first seven years, they learn through imitation. Any genuine art of education must fully respect this principle of imitation—otherwise, it is all too easy to misjudge our children's behavior.

To illustrate this point, let me give you an example, just one of hundreds that could be chosen. The father of a boy, aged about five, once came to me and told me that a very sad thing had happened; namely, that his boy had been stealing. I suggested that we begin by carefully examining whether in fact the child had really stolen. The father told me that the boy had taken money from the drawer where his wife kept it and had then bought candy with it, which he shared with other children in the street. I asked the father what usually happened with the money kept in the drawer. He replied that the boy's mother took the amount of money needed for the household that day out of her drawer every morning. Hearing this, I could reassure him that his boy had not stolen at all. I said, "The child is five years old. This means that he is still fully in the stage of imitation. Therefore, it is only good and proper that he should do what he sees done in his environment. His mother takes money out of the drawer every day, and so he naturally copies her. This is not stealing but merely behavior appropriate to the fundamental principle of a child's development during the first seven-year period."

A real teacher must know these things. During the first seven years of life, one cannot guide and direct a child by reprimands, nor by moral commands. During this period, one must guide a child by one's own deeds and by setting an example. But there are of course imponderables to be reckoned with in human as in outer nature. We guide a child not only with external deeds, but also with inner thoughts and feelings. If children enjoy the company of grown-ups who never allow unworthy thoughts or feelings to enter into their lives, something noble and good could become of them. On the other hand, if adults allow themselves mean, ignoble thoughts or feelings when they are around young people, believing that such thoughts or feelings do not matter since everyone is safely ensheathed within an individual bodily structure, they are mistaken, for such things do work on children. Imponderables are at work.

Such imponderables also manifest themselves in the second period of life, which begins after the change of teeth—when the child enters school—and lasts until the age of puberty, around fourteen. When we were working out the fundamentals of a truly spiritual-scientific, spiritually artistic pedagogy for the Waldorf school in Stuttgart—founded by Emil Molt and directed by myself—we had to make a special study of this transition from the first life period, that of imitation, to the second period, from the change of teeth to puberty. For all teaching, education, and upbringing at the Waldorf School is to be based entirely upon anthroposophical insight into human nature. And because children change from the stage of imitation into quite a different stage—I shall say more about this presently—we had to make a special effort to study this time of transition.

During the second period, leading up to puberty, imitation alone no longer suffices to form the faculties, the child's whole being. A new impulse now emerges from the depths of the child's soul. The child now wishes to regard the teacher as a figure of undisputed authority. Today, when everything goes under the banner of democracy, the demand is easily made that schools, too, should be "democratized." There are even those who would do away with the distinction between teacher and pupil altogether, advocating "community schools," or whatever name these bright ideas are given. Such ideas are a consequence of party-political attitudes, not knowledge of human nature. But educational questions should not be judged from partisan positions; they should be judged only on their own merits. And, if you do this, you will find that, between second dentition and puberty, a child is no longer obliged to imitate, but now has a deep desire to learn what is right or wrong, good or evil, from a beloved and naturally respected authority figure.

Happy are those who throughout their lives can remember such childhood authorities and can say of themselves, "I had a teacher. When I went to visit her, opening the door to her room, I already felt full of awe. To me, it was perfectly natural that my teacher was the source of everything good and true." Such things are not subject to argument on social or any other grounds. What is important is to gain the insight into human nature so that one can say, "Just as a young child's urge to play, which manifests in individually different ways, resurfaces as more or less skill in fitting into life when the young person is in his or her twenties, so another, similar transformation also occurs regarding a child's reverence for the teacher as a figure of authority. That is, only if faith in the authority of the adults in charge develops fully between the ages of approximately seven and fifteen will the right sense of freedom develop later, when the feeling for freedom must be the basis for all social life."

People cannot become free as adults unless they found as children support in the natural authority of adults. Likewise, only those who during the first period of life are allowed to pass through the process of adjusting themselves to their environment through the inborn desire to imitate can be motivated as adults to take a loving interest in the social sphere. This ability to adjust based on imitation does not last; what is needed in later life is a social awareness, the development of which depends on how far educators of children under seven can become worthy models of imitation. We need people today who are able to place themselves into life with a genuine sense of freedom. They are those who were able to look up to their educators and teachers as persons of authority during the time between their second dentition and puberty.

If one has stated publicly—as I already did in my book *Intuitive Thinking as a Spiritual Path*, published in 1892[3]—that the sense of freedom and the feeling for freedom are the basic facts of social life, one is hardly likely to speak against freedom and democracy. But, just because of this positive attitude towards freedom, one must also acknowledge that the practice of education as an art depends on the sense of authority, developed by the child during the second period of life. During this same period, the child also has to make a gradual transition from living in mental images—or pictures—to a more intellectual approach, a process that moves through and beyond another important turning point.

A true art of education must be able to penetrate such important issues.

---

3. Also translated as *The Philosophy of Freedom* or *The Philosophy of Spiritual Activity*.

The turning point to be discussed now occurs around a child's ninth year—but sometimes not before the tenth or even the eleventh year. [4] When our teachers recognize that a child is passing this point, they accompany the change with an appropriate change in pedagogy. In early childhood, a child learns to speak, gradually learning to refer to itself as "I". Up to the ninth year, however, the distinction between the child's "I" and the surrounding world is still rather undefined. Those who can observe things carefully recognize that the period when a child learns to differentiate between self and surroundings—approximately between the ninth and the eleventh years—is critical. It is a time when the child is actually crossing a Rubicon. The way in which the teachers respond to this change is of greatest importance for a child's future life. Teachers must have the right feeling for what is happening. They must realize that the child no longer experiences itself as an organic part of its environment—as a finger might experience itself as a part of the body if it had its own consciousness—but as a separate, independent entity. If they do so and respond in the right way as teachers, they can create a source of lasting joy and vitality in life. But if they fail to respond rightly, they open the way to barren and weary lives for their pupils later on. It is important to realize that, prior to this significant change, the child still lives in a world of pictures so closely related to its own nature that, unable to appreciate the difference between self and environment, it merges into its surroundings. Therefore, in assisting a child to establish its relationship to the world at this stage, a teacher must use a pictorial approach.

We receive the children into our school from their parental homes. Today, we live in an age when writing and reading have

---

4. On the nine-year-old turning point, see Hermann Koepke, *Encountering the Self.*

produced conventional symbols no longer bearing any direct inner relationship to the human being. Compare the abstract letters of our alphabet with the picture writing used in ages past. What was fixed into written forms in ancient times still bore a resemblance to people's mental images. But writing nowadays has become quite abstract. If we introduce children directly to these abstract letters in reading and writing lessons, we introduce them to something alien to their nature, or at least something inappropriate for six-, seven-, or eight-year olds. For this reason, we use a different method in our Waldorf school.

Instead of beginning with the letters of the alphabet, we engage our young pupils in artistic activity by letting them paint and draw; that is, work with colors and forms. In this activity, not only the head is engaged—which would have a very harmful effect—but the child's entire being is involved. We then let the actual letters emerge out of these color-filled forms. This is how our Waldorf pupils learn writing. They learn writing first. And only afterward do they learn to read, for printed letters are even more abstract than our handwritten ones. In other words, only gradually do we develop the abstract element, so necessary today, from the artistic element which is more closely allied to life. We proceed similarly in other subjects, too. And we work in this way toward a living, artistic pedagogy that makes it possible to reach the very soul of the child. As for the nature of what we usually think of as plant, mineral, and so forth, this can be fruitfully taught only after the child has passed the turning point just characterized and can differentiate itself from its surroundings.

Working along these lines, it might well happen that some of our pupils learn to read and write later than pupils in other schools. But this is no drawback. On the contrary, it is even an advantage. Of course, it is quite possible to teach young children reading and writing by rote and get them to rattle off what is put before their eyes, but it is also possible to deaden something in them by doing this, and anything killed during childhood remains dead for the rest of one's life. The opposite is equally true. What we allow to live and what we wake into life is the very stuff that will blossom and give life vitality. To nurture this process, surely, is the task of a real educator.

You will doubtless have heard of those educational ideas already published during the nineteenth century that emphasize the importance of activating a child's individuality. [5] We are told that, instead of cramming children with knowledge, we should bring out their inherent gifts and abilities. Certainly, no one would wish to denigrate such great geniuses of education. Important things have certainly been said by the science of education. On the other hand, though one can listen carefully to its abstract demands, such as that the individuality of the child should be developed, positive results will be achieved only if one is able to observe, day by day, how a child's individuality actually unfolds. One must know how, during the first seven years, the principle of imitation rules the day; how, during the following period from the seventh to the fourteenth year, the principle of authority predominates; and how this latter principle is twinned with the child's gradual transition from mental imagery—which is essentially of a pictorial or symbolic nature and based on memory—to the forming of concepts by the awakening intellect: a process that begins in the eleventh to twelfth year. If we can observe all of this and learn from a spiritual-scientific and artistic way of observing how to respond as a teacher, we shall achieve much more than if we attempt to follow an abstract aim, such as educating a

5. Above all, the Swiss educational reformer Johann Heinrich Pestalozzi (1746–1827) and Friedrich Wilhel August Fröbel (1782–1852), founder of the kindergarten system.

child out of its individuality. Spiritual science does not create abstractions, it does not make fixed demands; rather, it looks toward what can be developed into an art through spiritual perceptiveness and a comprehensive, sharpened sense of observation.

Last time, I was able to describe only briefly the kind of knowledge of the human being given by spiritual science that can form a basis for dealing with such practical matters as education. The pressing demands of society show clearly enough the need for such knowledge today. By complementing the outer, material aspects of life with supersensible and spiritual insights, spiritual science or anthroposophy leads us from a generally unreal, abstract concept of life to a concrete practical reality. According to this view, human beings occupy a central position in the universe. Such realistic understanding of human nature and human activities is what is needed today. Let me reinforce this point with a characteristic example.

Imagine that we wanted to convey a simple religious concept—for instance, the concept of the immortality of the human soul—to a class of young children. If we approach the subject pictorially, we can do this before a child's ninth year. For example, we can say, "Look at the butterfly's chrysalis. Its hard shell cracks open and the butterfly flutters out into the air. A similar thing happens when a human being dies. The immortal soul dwells in the body. But, when death breaks it open, just as the butterfly flies from the chrysalis into the air, so the soul flies away from the dead body into the heavenly world, only the human soul remains invisible."

When we study such an example from the point of view of a living art of education, we come face to face with life's imponderables. A teacher might have chosen such a comparison by reasoning somewhat as follows: "I am the one who knows, for I am much older than the child. I have thought out this picture of the caterpillar and the butterfly because of the child's ignorance and immaturity. As someone of superior intelligence, I have made the child believe something in which I myself do not believe. In fact, from my own point of view, it was only a silly little story, invented solely for the purpose of getting the child to understand the concept of the immortality of the soul." If this is a teacher's attitude, he or she will achieve but little. Although to say this might sound paradoxical in our materialistic age, it is nevertheless true: if teachers are insincere, their words do not carry much weight.

To return to our example. If Waldorf teachers had chosen this comparison for their classes, the situation, though outwardly similar, would have been very different. For they would not have used it—nor, for that matter, any other picture or simile—unless they were convinced of its inherent truth. A Waldorf teacher, an anthroposophically oriented spiritual researcher, would not feel, "I am the intelligent adult who makes up a story for the children's benefit," but rather: "The eternal beings and powers, acting as the spiritual in nature, have placed before my eyes a picture of the immortal human soul, objectively, in the form of the emerging butterfly. Believing in the truth of this picture with every fibre of my being, and bringing it to my pupils through my own conviction, I will awaken in them a truly religious concept. What matters is not so much what I, as teacher, say to the child, but what I am and what my heartfelt attitude is." These are the kinds of things that must be taken more and more seriously in the art of education.

You will also understand when I tell you that visitors to our Waldorf school, who come to see the school in action and to observe lessons, cannot see the whole. It is almost as if, for instance, you cut a small piece out of a Rembrandt painting, believing that you could gain an overall impression of the whole picture through it. Such a thing is not possible when an impulse is conceived and practiced as a comprehensive whole—as the Waldorf school is—and when it is rooted in the totality of anthroposophical spiritual science.

You might have been wondering which kind of people would make good teachers in such a school. They are people whose entire lives have been molded by the spiritual knowledge of which I spoke last time. The best way of learning to know the Waldorf school and of becoming familiar with its underlying principles is by gaining knowledge of anthroposophical spiritual science itself at least as a first step. A few short visits in order to observe lessons will hardly convey an adequate impression of Waldorf pedagogy.

Plain speaking in such matters is essential, because it points toward the character of the new spirit that, flowing from the High School of Spiritual Science centered in Dornach, is to enter all practical spheres of life—social, artistic, educational, and so forth.

If you consider thoroughly all that I have been telling you, you will no longer think it strange that those who enter more deeply into the spirit underlying this art of education find it absolutely essential to place themselves firmly upon the ground of a free spiritual life. Because education has become dependent on the state on the one hand and on the economic sphere on the other, there is a tendency for it to become abstract and programmatic. Those who believe in the anthroposophical way of life must insist on a free and independent cultural-spiritual life. This represents one of the three branches of the threefold social order about which I wrote in my book *The Threefold Commonwealth*.[6]

---

6. *Die Kernpunkte der Sozialen Frage*, 1919, GA23. For the threefold social order, see also (among others) *The Renewal of the Social Organism*; and *The Social Future*.

One of the demands that must be made for spiritual life—something that is not at all utopian, that may be begun any day—is that those actively engaged in spiritual life (and this means, above all, those involved in its most important public domain; namely, education) should also be entrusted with all administrative matters, and this in a broad and comprehensive way.

The maximum number of lessons to be taught—plus the hours spent on other educational commitments—should allow teachers sufficient time for regular meetings, in both smaller and larger groups, to deal with administrative matters. However, only practicing teachers—not former teachers now holding state positions or retired teachers—should be called on to care for this side of education. For what has to be administered in each particular school—as in all institutions belonging to the spiritual-cultural life—should be only a continuation of what is being taught, of what forms the content of every word spoken and every deed performed in the classroom. Rules and regulations must not be imposed from outside the school. In spiritual life, autonomy, self-administration, is essential.

I am well aware that people who like to form logical "quickly tailored" concepts, as well as others who, somewhat superficially, favor a more historical perspective, will readily object to these ideas. But in order to recognize the necessity of making spiritual-cultural life into a free and independent member of the social organism, one really must be acquainted with its inherent nature. Anyone who has been a teacher at a working-class adult-education center for several years—as I was in the school founded by Wilhelm Liebknecht,[7] thereby gaining firsthand

7. Wilhelm Liebknecht, 1826–1900, founder of the German Social-Democratic Party. The school was a Worker's College. Rudolf Steiner taught history, public speaking, and composition there.

experience of the social question—knows only too well that this is not merely a matter of improving external arrangements or of dealing with dissatisfaction caused by unjust outer conditions. As I say, if one has taught in such circles, one knows that one word comes up repeatedly in proletarian circles, but extends far beyond proletarian life, namely, the word *"ideology,"* the meaning of which is set out in the first chapter of *The Threefold Commonwealth*. Now, what is hidden behind this?

Long ago, in the ancient East, people spoke of the great illusion or *"maya."* According to this view—already decadent today and hence unsuited to our Western ways—*maya* refers to the external sensory world which offers us only semblance or outer appearance. To ancient sages, true reality of being—the reality that sustained human beings—lived and grew in the soul. All else, all that the outer senses beheld, was only *maya*.

We live today in an age that expresses—especially in its most radical philosophies—a total reversal of this ancient view. For most people today true reality resides in outer, physical nature and in the processes of production, while what can be found inwardly in the human soul as morality, art, religion, knowledge is *maya, illusion*. If we want to translate the word maya correctly, we must translate it as "ideology." For modern humanity, all other translations fail. But ideology refers to exactly the opposite of what *maya* was for the ancient oriental. The widest circles of the population today call *maya* what the ancient oriental called the sole reality. And this reversal of the word's meaning is of great significance for life today.

I have known people of the leading classes who lived under the influence of the philosophy that gave rise to ideology. I have learned to know the perplexity of people who reasoned thus: if we trust what natural science tells us, the entire origin of the cosmos can be traced to a primeval nebula. According to these theories, all of the different species of nature began during this stage.

At that time, too, human beings densified out of the nebula. And, while this process continued, something not unlike soap bubbles unfolded in the human soul. According to natural science, what rises in the human soul as ethics, religion, science or art, does not represent reality. Indeed, if we look toward the end of earthly evolution as it is presented by science, all that is offered is the prospect of an immense cemetery. On earth, death would follow, due either to general glaciation, or to total annihilation by heat. In either case, the result would be a great cemetery for all human ideals—for everything considered to be the essence of human values and the most important aspect of human existence. If we are honest in accepting what natural science tells us—such people had to conclude—then all that remains is only a final extinction of all forms of existence.

I have witnessed the sense of tragedy and the deep-seated pain in the souls of such materialistically minded members of today's leading circles, who could not escape the logical conclusions of the natural-scientific outlook and who were consequently forced to look on all that is most precious in the human beings as mere illusion. In many people, I have seen this pessimism, which was a result of their honest pursuit of the natural-scientific conception of the world.

This attitude took a special form in the materialism of the working class. There, everything of a spiritual nature is generally looked upon as a kind of a superstructure, as mere smoke or fog; in a word, as "ideology". And what enters and affects the soul condition of modern people in this way is the actual source of the contemporary anti-social sentiment—however many other reasons might be constantly invented and published. They amount only to a form of self deception. It is the influence of this attitude which is the real origin of the dreadful catastrophes that are dawning—undreamt of by most people—in the whole East. So far, they have started in Russia, where they have already assumed devastating proportions. They will assume even greater dimensions unless steps are taken to replace an ideology by a living grasp of the spirit.

Anthroposophical spiritual science gives us not only ideas and concepts of something real but also ideas and concepts by which we know that we are not just *thinking about* something filled with spirit. Spiritual science gives us the living spirit itself, not just spirit in the form of thoughts. It shows human beings as beings filled with living spirit—just like the ancient religions. Like the ancient religions, the message of spiritual science is not just "you will know something," but "you will know something, and divine wisdom will thereby live in you. As blood pulses in you, so by true knowing will divine powers too pulse in you." Spiritual science, as represented in Dornach, wishes to bring to humanity precisely such knowledge and spiritual life.

To do so, we need the support of our contemporaries. Working in small ways will not lead to appropriate achievements. What is needed is work on a large scale. Spiritual science is free from sectarianism. It has the will to carry out the great tasks of our times, including those in the practical spheres of life. But to bring this about, spiritual science must be understood in a living way by contemporary society. It is not enough to open a few schools here and there, modeled on the Waldorf school, as some people wish. This is not the way forward, for it will not lead to greater freedom in spiritual life.

Often, I have had to suffer the painful experience of witnessing the conduct of certain people who, because of their distrust in orthodox, materialistic medicine, approached me, trying to tempt me into quackery. They wanted to be cured by creeping through the back door, as it were. I have experienced it to the point of revulsion. There was, for instance, a Prussian government official, who publicly supported materialistic medicine in parliament, granting it sole rights, only to enter by the back door to be treated by the very people whom he had opposed most violently in parliament.

The Anthroposophical Society—which could, from a certain point of view, be justly described as willing to make sacrifices and whose members have dedicated themselves to the cultivation of anthroposophical spiritual science—seeks a powerful impetus, capable of affecting and working into the world at large. What is at issue today is nothing less than the following—that a true spiritual life, such as our present society needs, can be created only by those interested in it, which fundamentally includes everyone, many of whom have children, and that these must bring about the right conditions in which children can mature into free human beings so that those children, in turn, can create an existence worthy of humanity. As far as spiritual-cultural life is concerned, everyone is an interested party and should do his or her share to work for what the future will provide in the form of spiritual-cultural life.

Thus, what I would like to call "a world school movement," based on the ideas I have put forward today, should meet with approval in the widest quarters. What really ought to happen is that all those who can clearly see the need for a free spiritual-cultural life should unite to form an international world school movement. An association of that kind would offer a stronger and more-living impetus for uniting nations than many other associations being founded these days on the basis of old and abstract principles. Such a union of nations, spiritually implied in a world school movement, could be instrumental in uniting peoples all over the globe by their participation in this great task.

The modern state school system superseded the old denominational schools relatively recently. It was good and right that this happened. And yet, what was a blessing at the time when the state took this step would cease to be one if state-controlled education were to become permanent; for then, inevitably, education would become the servant of the state. The state can train theologians, lawyers, or other professionals to become its civil servants, but if the spiritual life is to be granted full independence, all persons in a teaching capacity must be responsible solely to the spiritual world, to which they can look up in the light of anthroposophically oriented spiritual science.

A world school movement, as I envisage it, would have to be founded on an entirely international basis by all who understand the meaning of a truly free spiritual life and what our human future demands in social questions. Gradually, such a world school movement would give birth to the general opinion that schools must be granted independence from the state and that the teachers in each school must be given the freedom to deal with that school's own administration. We must not be narrow minded or pedantic in these matters, as many are who doubt that enough parents would send their children to such schools. That is the wrong kind of thinking. One must be clear that freedom from state interference in education will be the call of the future. Even if there are objections from some parents, ways and means will have to be found for getting children to attend school without coercion by the state. Instead of opposing the founding of independent schools because of dissenting parents, ways and means will have to be found of helping free schools to come into existence despite possible opposition or criticisms—which must then be overcome in an appropriate way. I am convinced that the founding of a world school movement is of the greatest importance for the social development of humanity. Far and wide, it will awaken a sense for a real and practical free spiritual life. Once such a mood becomes universal, there will be no need to open Waldorf schools tucked away in obscure corners and existing at the mercy of governments, but governments will be forced into recognizing them fully and refraining from any interference, as long as these schools are truly founded in a free spiritual life.

What I have said so far about freedom in the cultural-spiritual sphere of life—namely that it has to create its own forms of existence—applies equally to the social sphere known by spiritual science as *the sphere of economic life.* Just as the sphere of cultural spiritual life must be formed on the basis of the capacities of every individual, so too must economic life be formed on the basis of its own principles, different though these are. Fundamentally, such economic principles derive from the fact that, in economics, a judgment made by an individual cannot be translated directly into deeds, into economic actions. In the cultural-spiritual sphere, we recognize that human souls strive for wholeness, for inner harmony. Teachers and educators must take that wholeness into account. They approach a child with that wholeness as their aim. In the economic sphere, on the other hand, we can be competent in a professional sense only in narrower, more specialized areas. In economics, therefore, it is only when we join together with people working in other areas that something fruitful may be achieved. In other words, just as free spiritual-cultural life emerged as one member of the threefold social organism, so likewise must economic life, based upon the associative principle, arise as another, independent member of this same threefold organism. In the future, economic life will be run on a basis quite different from what we are used to out of the past.

Economic life today is organized entirely according to past practices, for there is no other yardstick for earnings and profits. Indeed, people are not yet ready to contemplate a change in the economic system which is still entirely motivated by profit. I would like to clarify this by an example that, though perhaps not yet representing purely and simply the economic sphere, nevertheless has its economic aspects. It shows how the associative principle can be put into practice in the material realm.

There is, as you know, the Anthroposophical Society.[8] It might well be that there are many people who are not particularly fond of it and regard it as sectarian, which it certainly is not. Or they may be under the impression that it dabbles in nebulous mysticism, which again is not the case. Rather, it devotes itself to the cultivation of anthroposophical spiritual science. Many years ago, this Society founded the Philosophic-Anthroposophic Publishing Company in Berlin. To be exact, two people who were in harmony with the Anthroposophical Society's mode of thinking founded it.[9] This publishing company, however, does not work as other profit-making companies, which are the offspring of modern economic thinking, do. And how do these profit-making enterprises work? They print books. This means that so and so many people have to be employed for processing paper; so and so many compositors, printers, bookbinders; and so on. But now I ask you to look at those strange and peculiar products that make their appearance every year and which are called "crabs" in the book trade. These are newly printed books, which have not been purchased by the book sellers and which, consequently, at the next Easter Fair wander back to the publishers to be pulped. Here we have a case where wares have been put on the market, the production of which had occupied a whole host of workers, but all to no avail.

---

8. The Anthroposophical Society was founded on February 3, 1913. Until then, Rudolf Steiner had worked under the auspices of the German Section of the Theosophical Society. The Anthroposophical Society was refounded in 1923/24. As such, it still exists, headquartered in Dornach, Switzerland, with national societies throughout the world. For information on the Anthroposophical Society in America, write: 529 West Grant Place, Chicago, Illinois 60614.

9. Marie von Sivers (1867–1948)—later Frau Dr. Steiner—and Johanna Mücke (1864–1949).

Such unnecessary and purposeless expenditure of labor represents one important aspect of the social question. Nowadays, because one prefers to live with phrases rather than an objective understanding, there is too much talk about "unearned income."[10] It would be better to look at the situation more realistically, for similar situations arise in all branches of our external, material life. Until now, the Philosophic-Anthroposophic Publishing Company has not printed one single copy in vain. At most, there are a few books that were printed out of courtesy to our members. That was our conscious motive; they were printed as a kind of offering to those members. Otherwise there was always a demand for whatever we printed. Our books always sold out quickly and nothing was printed unnecessarily. Not a single worker's time was wasted and no useless labor was performed within the social framework. A similar situation could be achieved in the whole economic sphere if one organized cooperation between *consumers* who have an understanding of needs and demands in a particular domain, *traders* who trade in certain products, and last, the actual *producers*. Consumers, traders, and producers would form an association whose main task would be the fixing of prices. Such associations would have to determine their own size; if they grew too large, they would no longer be cost effective. Such associations could then unite to form larger associations. They could expand into what might be called global or world-economic associations—for the characteristic feature of recent economics is its expansion of economies into a world economy.

A great deal more would have to be said to give an adequate account of what I can indicate here only in principle. I must,

10. "Unearned income" is the literal translation of "erwerbsloses Einkommen." Seen in its context, Rudolf Steiner seems to refer to income from non-social activities.

however, say that the concept of associative life implies nothing organizational. In fact, although I come from Germany (and have lived there frequently even though my main sphere of activity is now Dornach, Switzerland) the mere word "organization" produces a thoroughly distasteful effect in me. "Organization" implies an ordering from above, from a center. This is something that economic life cannot tolerate. Because the Middle-European states, penned in between the West and the East, were trying to plan their economies, they were actually working against a healthy form of economic life. The associative principle which must be striven for in economics leaves industry, as also industrial cooperatives, to their own devices. It only links them together according to levels of production and consumption regulated by the activity of the administrators of the various associations. This is done through free agreements among single individuals or various associations.

A more detailed description of this subject can be found in my book *The Threefold Commonwealth*, or in other of my writings, such as *The Renewal of the Social Organism*, which is supplementary to *The Threefold Commonwealth.*

Thus, in order to meet the needs of our times, anthroposophical spiritual science, based on practical life experience, calls for two independent members of the social organism—a free spiritual life and an associative economic life. Those two are essential in the eyes of anyone seriously and honestly concerned about one of the fundamental longings in the hearts of our contemporaries; namely, the longing for democracy.

Dear friends, I spent the first half of my life in Austria—thirty years—and have seen with my own eyes what it means not to take seriously society's heartfelt demand for democracy.[11] In the

11. For an account of Rudolf Steiner's life, see his *Autobiography* and Stewart Easton, *Rudolf Steiner: Herald of a New Epoch.*

1860s, the call for parliamentarianism was heard in Austria, too. But because it could not bring about the right social conditions, this land of political experimentation was the first to go under in the last great World War. A parliament was formed. But how was it constituted? It was composed of four assemblies: landowners, the chamber of commerce, the department of towns, markets and industrial areas, and, finally, the assembly of country parishes. In other words, only economic interests were represented. There were thus four departments, each dealing with various aspects of the national economy. Together, they constituted the Austrian Parliament, where they were supposed to come to decisions regarding political and legal matters as well as matters pertaining to general affairs of the state. This means that all decisions, reached by majority vote, represented only economic interests. Such majorities, however, can never make fruitful contributions to the social development of humanity. Nor are they the outcome of any expert knowledge. Truly, the call for democracy, for human freedom, demands honesty.

At the same time, however, one must also be clear that only certain issues are suitable for parliamentary procedures, and that democracy is appropriate only when the issues treated lie within the areas of responsibility of each person of voting age. Thus, between free spiritual life on one side and associative economic life on the other, the sphere of *democracy* becomes the third member of the threefold social organism. This democratic sphere represents the political sphere of rights within the social organism. Here each individual meets the other on equal terms. For instance, in such questions as the number of working hours and the rights of workers in general, each person of age must be considered competent to judge.

Let us move toward a future in which questions of cultural and spiritual life are decided freely and entirely within their own sphere, a future in which freedom in education is striven for so that schools can work out of the spirit and, consequently, produce skillful, practical people. Then, practical schools, too, will develop from such a free spiritual life. Let us move toward a future in which spiritual life is allowed to work within its own sphere and in which the powers of the state are limited to what lies within the areas of responsibility of each person of voting age; a future in which economic life is structured according to the principle of associations, where judgments are made collectively on the strength of the various members' expertise and where agreements are made with others who are experts in their fields. If we approach the future with these aims in mind, we shall move toward a situation that will be very different from what many people, unable to adapt themselves to new conditions, imagine today.

There will be many who believe that a nebulous kind of cultural spiritual life, alienated from ordinary life, emanates from Dornach. But such is not the case at all. However absurd it may sound, according to the spirit prevailing in Dornach, no one can be a proper philosopher who does not also know how to chop wood or dig potatoes. In short, according to this spirit, one cannot be a philosopher if one cannot turn a hand to tasks requiring at least a modicum of practical skill. Spiritual science does not estrange people from practical life; on the contrary, it helps them develop skills in coping with life. It is not abstract. It is a reality, penetrating human beings with real strength. It therefore not only increases people's thinking activity, it also makes them generally more skillful. At the same time, spiritual science is intimately connected to a sense of inner dignity and morality; that is, to morality, religion, and art. Visitors to the Goetheanum can convince themselves of this—although the building is not finished yet by any means. Indeed, in order to bring it even into its present state, people with an understanding for the impulse it embodies have already made many sacrifices. The

Goetheanum is not a result of our employing the services of an architect and a builder to erect a building in a more or less conventional style—be it in Gothic, Renaissance, or any other style. The living quality of the science of the spirit spoken of here could not have tolerated that. Spiritual science had to evolve its own style in keeping with its own nature. This manifests in the various artistic forms. Just as the same growth forces that produce a nut's kernel also form its shell—for the shell can be formed only by the same principle as also works in the kernel—so the outer shell of our building, the center of what is being willed in Dornach, can arise only from the same spiritual sources from which all of the teaching and researching in Dornach also flows. The words spoken there and the results of research conducted there all proceed from the same sources as the artistic forms of the building's pillars and the paintings inside the cupolas. All of the sculpture, architectural design, and painting—and these are not empty symbolism or allegories—arise from the same spiritual impulses that underlie all of the teaching and researching. And, because all this is part of the one cultural-spiritual life that we hope to quicken in the human being, the third, *religious* element, is closely linked to the arts and to science, forming a unity with them.

In other words, what we are striving for as spiritual science—as it enters into the practical spheres of life as the "threefolding" (or tripartition) of the social organism—brings to realization the three great ideals that resound from the eighteenth century in such a heart-rending, spirit-awakening way. I refer to the threefold call to humanity: freedom, equality, brotherhood. Learned people in the nineteenth century pointed out repeatedly that it was impossible for those three ideals to be put into practice simultaneously under any one state or government. Such was their considered opinion and, from their point of view, justifiably so. But the apparent incongruity rests on false premises. Freedom, equality, and brotherhood do resound to us from the eighteenth century as the three great and justly-claimed ideals. The source of misunderstanding is the tacit assumption that the state must be given sole prerogative in matters pertaining to all three spheres of society. The thought never occurred that, in accord with its own nature, such a monolithic state should be membered into three social organisms: the free *spiritual* organism; the organism representing the *sphere of politics and rights*, built on equality; and the organism of the *economic* sphere, built on the principle of association.

Objections have been raised against these views by people who expect to be taken seriously in social questions and who maintain that, by demanding a tripartition of society, I seek to destroy its unity. But the unity of the human organism is not destroyed because it naturally consists of three parts. Nor is the unity of the human being disturbed because the blood, as it circulates rhythmically through the body, is sustained by a part of the organism different from the one in which the nerves are centered. Likewise, the unity of the social organism is enhanced rather than disturbed by recognition of its threefold nature (if the human head, apart from sending forth the nerves, would also have to produce the blood, then the unity of the human organism would certainly be destroyed). All of this is explained in much greater detail in my book *Riddles of the Soul.*[12]

I would like to conclude these considerations about spiritual science and its practical application in social life by pointing out that, although the three great ideals of humanity—liberty, equality, fraternity—are not realizable within the framework of an all-powerful state monopoly—where any attempted implementation would be founded upon illusion—they can nevertheless penetrate human life in the form of a threefold ordering of

12. *Riddles of the Soul* (1917); English edition, *The Case for Anthroposophy.*

society. Here, the following order would prevail: full freedom in the cultural-spiritual sphere; equality in the realm where each person of voting age shares in democratic rights and responsibilities on equal terms with fellow citizens of voting age; and brotherhood in the economic sphere which will be realized by means of the principle of associations. Unity will not be destroyed by this ordering, for every human being stands in all three spheres, forming a living link toward unity.

Basically, one may consider the meaning of world evolution to reside in the fact that the particular ways of its working and its underlying forces culminate in the human being as the apex of the entire world organism. Just as the forces of nature and the entire cosmos—the macrocosm—are to be found again on a minute scale in the microcosm, in the threefold human being, so the great ideals—liberty, equality, and fraternity—must come together again in the social organism. But this must not be brought about by external or abstract means: it must proceed in accordance with reality, so that these three ideals can work in harmony with the human nature in its integral unity. As free individuals, every human being can share in the free spiritual life to which all belong. Sharing equal rights with our fellow citizens, we can all participate in the democratic life of the state, based on the principle of equality. Finally, by participating in economic life, we share in the brotherhood of all human beings.

Liberty in the cultural spiritual sphere; *equality* in political life and the sphere of rights; *fraternity* in economic life. These three working together harmoniously will lead to the healing and further evolution of humanity—to new resources in the struggle against the forces of decline.

A combination of these three in a genuine social organism, a concurrence of freedom, equality, and brotherhood in integral human nature—this appears to be the magical password for the future of humanity.

3

Knowledge of Health and Illness in Education

DORNACH — SEPTEMBER 26, 1921

The education that has arisen from the whole anthroposophical understanding of the world—which is being put into practice in the Waldorf school in Stuttgart and other, smaller schools organized on the same principles—has to be far more comprehensive than the forms of education usual today. Above all, it has to be far more closely linked to knowledge of human beings as a whole. Once what we call anthroposophical education is properly understood, we will speak of it not so much as an objective pedagogical science or art but rather, and more importantly, as a way of understanding the whole human being. We shall speak of it in terms of the growing, unfolding child who is to be educated. And we shall know more about what one human being can mean to another and particularly what the teacher means to the pupil.

The important relationship of one human being to another existing between teacher and pupil has suffered from the tendency toward specialization that has increasingly entered all work and striving in the cultural-spiritual sphere in recent times. Specialization has gone so far that it is now believed that it is not only teachers who should influence the growing child. Since schools have to deal with the healthy or unhealthy ways in which children develop, it is now thought that the physician too should exert an influence in school. And, in most recent times, it is even considered necessary for a qualified psychologist, who has acquired specialized knowledge of the human soul by the usual methods, to be present to advise the teachers. We thus see teachers receiving advice from medical doctors on one side and from psychologists on the other. This is nothing but an introduction of specialization into the life of the school.

But if we understand correctly the close relationship that has to form between the teacher and the child who is to be educated, and understand how intimately the teacher must know what is actually happening in the growing child, then we can hardly favor such superficial forms of cooperation among people who are thrown together only by outward circumstances, each understanding only one aspect of human development. We will not think it helpful that such persons should contribute their advice in order to bring about an external form of cooperation. What is emerging here, then, is but a consequence of specialization as such. Of course, those who believe that the human soul has only an external relationship to the physical, bodily organism might believe that it is the teacher's task to deal only with the child's soul and that the doctor is there to give advice regarding the physical aspect of education.

It goes without saying that, though I shall speak of the importance of the teacher's knowledge of health and illness in education, I am not referring to acute or chronic illnesses in pupils. Naturally, medical treatment in such cases lies outside the province of education. In what follows, therefore, I shall confine myself to what belongs to the general field of education. I must here state clearly that, if people believe that the doctor, as a specialist, must assist the teachers in matters of hygiene in a school, then they are encouraging a tendency to onesidedness in the principles and the practice of education:

they are separating and alienating from each other two sides of what constitute a natural whole in childhood—children's souls and spirits on one hand and their physical-bodily nature on the other.

Depending in this way on the help of specialists—leaving physical questions in the hands of the specialists—drives educational theory and practice into abstraction. Confirming this tendency, matters have now gone so far that great surprise is shown in many quarters when one fails to conform one's pedagogy and actual teaching to the usual abstract rules and regulations, but rather adapts them to conform to the totality of the human being, which naturally also includes the physical aspects. This aberration, as I may call it, is due to the fact that science nowadays no longer has any clear understanding of the relationship of soul and spirit to the physical-bodily aspect—if science speaks of soul and spirit as having any independent existence at all.

Clear evidence of this is shown by contemporary psychology's frequent references to a "psycho-physical parallelism." Psychologists feel that they must speak about human soul and spirit; but they also feel it necessary to speak about the physical aspects of the human being. However, since they no longer recognize the living interplay between soul and spirit and body, they speak of "parallelism"—as if there were spiritual phenomena on one side and, beside them, physical and bodily phenomena on the other, the two running side by side. But the way in which those two interact and interweave is naturally altogether neglected.

This external way of looking at the relationship between soul-spiritual and bodily aspects of the human being has slowly colored the theory and practice of education. Here one thing must be made clear. This is something that I can describe only by referring to anthroposophy in general. I refer to the fact that if we speak of the bodily, physical aspect of a living human being as contemporary physiology and biology do, then we are speaking about something that, in reality, does not exist in the form in which we are speaking of it—because the entire physical part of a human being is a result, a synthesis of the soul and spiritual aspects.

Furthermore, if we speak about soul and spirit in the abstract, we are not speaking about something real either. Soul and spirit live in the living human being where they permeate, build up, and shape the physical body. This means that it is not possible to speak of the relationship of soul and spirit to the physical body in general terms. Once we can see soul and spirit in their configuration—not merely in the abstract, but as they are inwardly structured—we know that every detail of soul and spirit is related in a specific way to every detail of our bodily and physical nature. If, for example, we observe the process of seeing, we find its physical and bodily location isolated in the human head, and can study the process of seeing by studying its localized organs in the head. But we find a different situation if we study the process of hearing. To study hearing, we must also study the rhythmic system. In fact, to understand the process of hearing, we must begin with the process of breathing. One cannot study hearing as if its seat were localized, isolated, in the head, as is often done in today's abstract physiology. The same principle holds good for the whole of physiology. We must relate soul and spirit to definite organic systems when we study them. This means that a real understanding of soul and spirit is quite impossible without knowledge of the bodily and physical nature and vice versa. Comprehensive knowledge of physical nature is knowledge of soul and spirit. Although from the present-day perspective what is soul -spiritual and what is physical appear to part company, at most running parallel to each other, we must strive for a way of knowing that unites the soul-spiritual and physical-bodily natures in the living human being.

Members of this audience who have come to listen to these lectures because of their interest in anthroposophy know that here we do not speak of soul and spirit abstractly or theoretically. They know that in anthroposophy, knowledge of soul and spirit is truly experienced and fully and intimately interwoven with knowledge of the physical-bodily aspects.

Now, once we consider the bodily and physical aspects of the human being, we are immediately faced with the question of the relationship of health and illnesses. Extreme cases of illness, as I said, certainly do not belong to the field of education. Yet the manifold tendencies toward illness to be found in 1,001 different ways in a so-called healthy human being constitutes an area that ought to be known thoroughly by those who wish to become educators. This is an extremely important area of pedagogical knowledge. In order to make clear what I mean, let me refer to a very important concept in Goethe's world-view.[1]

In his theory of metamorphosis, Goethe tried to gain an understanding of organic life. And his achievements in the field of metamorphosis will certainly find greater and more unprejudiced approval in the future than has been the case so far, because present trends in science have often gone in the direction opposite to Goethe's approach. To take the simplest example, Goethe observed how, when leaf upon leaf develops along the stem of a plant, each successive leaf, which shows a different

---

1. For Rudolf Steiner on Goethe, see, among others: *Goethean Science* (Spring Valley, New York: Mercury Press, 1988), *Science of Knowing* (The Theory of Knowledge Implicit in Goethe's World Conception) (Spring Valley, New York: Mercury Press, 1988), *Goethe's World View* (Spring Valley, New York: Mercury Press, 1985), and *Nature's Open Secret: Rudolf Steiner and Goethe's Participatory Approach to Science* (Hudson, New York: Anthroposophic Press, forthcoming).

shape from the leaf below, is in fact nothing but a metamorphosis of the lower leaf. According to Goethe, the separate organs of the plant—the simpler, lower leaves, then the more complicated leaves on the stem, followed by the sepals which again are shaped quite differently from the leaves, and the petals which have even a different color from that of the leaves on the stem—all differ outwardly in form but inwardly follow the same underlying pattern. In other words, an identical idea assumes manifold forms and designs in outer appearance.

This insight allowed Goethe to see the whole plant in the leaf and, likewise, only complex variations of a single leaf in the whole plant. For Goethe, each leaf is a whole plant. The idea of the plant, the type of the plant—the archetypal plant—assumes a definite form in outward physical appearance; it becomes simplified, and so on. Goethe said that, when it produces a leaf, the stem really wants to grow a whole plant. The inherent tendency to do this definitely exists, but the force that could produce a plant develops only to a limited degree; it is held back in the leaf. And, in the next leaf, it unfolds again only to a limited degree, and so on. In each leaf, a whole plant wants to unfold—the formative force strives to become a whole plant—but, in each case, only a fragment of a plant comes into existence. Yet the whole plant exists. It is a reality. And this invisible whole plant holds together in harmony what strives to become many different plants. Every plant wants to become many plants but does not succeed, developing only a limited formation, an organ. And every organ really wants to become an entire plant with the task of balancing the various individual, fragmentary formations for the sake of a greater harmony. This picture of metamorphosis shows us a force working developmentally in each individual organ, while limiting each organ's developmental growth and integrating the individual organs to form the overall whole of the complete plant.

Now, Goethe was never interested in formulating abstract concepts. He did not, for instance, coin an abstract concept such as, "one sees single, fragmentary plants wanting to develop and the unifying plant that holds them all together." That would be an abstraction. Goethe wants to know how the plant-forming force *works*. He wants to learn what it is that shapes itself in this way and, above all, what holds itself back in a single leaf. He wants to get a clear picture of this; he does not want to remain with only a concept. He wants to reach a living picture. Hence, what he called the "malformations" or "monstrosities" of a plant assumed great importance for him—such as when, on a definite part of a plant where one would expect to find a leaf, there is no leaf but the stem instead thickens and a malformation occurs; or when a blossom, instead of rounding itself off into petals, grows slim; and so on.

Goethe concluded that, where malformations occur in a plant, the plant-forming force reveals outwardly what it was meant to hold back. Where a leaf shows a malformation, that force was not held back but shot directly into the leaf. From this, Goethe realized that, when a malformation occurs, something that really belongs to the spiritual realm becomes physical. We see something become visible that was meant to be held back as a growth force. Hence, there is material for study in malformations, for malformations allow us to see what is active in the plant. Where such malformations do not occur, something is restrained that reveals itself later in the subsequent leaves or the other organs that follow.

For Goethe, then, malformations assume a special significance, extending to the study of the whole organism. In this sense, we are following in Goethe's footsteps when we consider, for instance, a hydrocephalic child, suffering from dropsy of the brain. Here, we have a malformation. Goethe would say, "If rightly studied, this malformation shows me something that exists as a tendency in every child's head but is normally held back within the spiritual sphere. Therefore, if such a malformation occurs, I can conclude that something is revealed there in the physical, sense-perceptible world that really belongs rightly to the soul-spiritual realm."

If we now look at a human being or an animal, we find not only such outwardly perceptible malformations but also illnesses or at least tendencies toward illnesses. According to Goethe's view, each illness reveals something living in each human being that develops onesidedly—like a malformation—while it ought to be held back within the entire organic system. Instead of remaining within the spiritual sphere, it strikes through into an external manifestation. We can say that, if we detect a tendency toward a certain illness somewhere, that very tendency reveals something of special significance regarding the human organization. Hence, when we understand illnesses, we really have a chance to study the human spirit by means of them, just as Goethe studied malformations to understand plant types and the archetypal plant. It is of greatest significance to be able to look at the more subtle weaknesses in each child, those subtle tendencies that do not deteriorate into gross illnesses but manifest as predispositions toward one or the other extreme, becoming illnesses there. This is a kind of outer indication of what is at work in every healthy human being. We could almost say that there is a hidden hydrocephaloid in every child. We must be able therefore to study hydrocephalic children in order to discover how to treat what has worked (like a malformation) too far into the physical sphere from the soul spiritual sphere in which it belongs. Naturally, this is something that must be treated with great scientific delicacy; it is not something to be coarsely interpreted. Considerable tact and careful, precise, scientific discrimination are needed here. For we are dealing with something at work in human beings, manifesting in this case as an illness but which, if it remains in its own proper inner sphere, belongs with children's normal developmental forces.

Since a child undergoes a constant process of growth and has tendencies toward all kinds of illness, you yourselves will be able to appreciate how, with the necessary knowledge of where those tendencies might lead, we can also become capable of harmonizing them, of calling forth counterforces when there is a danger of a child's falling into imbalance.

There is another point to be considered. Usually, when people talk of the theory and the practice of education, they feel that they must uphold an ideal that they can then elaborate in great theoretical detail. This approach, however, can lead to rigid forms and fixed claims. When one has to deal with pedagogical questions and when, as I was for instance, one is asked to guide the Waldorf school, a thought strikes one again and again. On the whole, audiences like to hear talks about education which seem to make sense to them. People like such talks. And, indeed, anyone who is scrupulously honest—and anthroposophy must always be scrupulously honest—can't help feeling: "There certainly is a need for our new education." And people, hearing about it, come and say, "This is wonderful. If only we could have gone to a school like the Waldorf school!" But, so often, the very people who want to pioneer educationally in this new way are the very ones who had to go through the worst forms of education themselves. They may have had to put up with the worst, most corrupt forms of education in their own schooling. And yet, in spite of their negative experiences, they are able to call for improved educational systems. Then the idea might strike one: does one really have the right to plan and think out, right down to specific details, how children should be educated? Would it not be better by far to let them grow up wild, as many biographies testify, telling us of persons who were not pressed into any particular educational mold, but nevertheless matured into most capable and responsible people? Do we not sin against the growing child if we present a pedagogical system that has been worked out down to the finest detail?

You see how you have to weigh everything in your mind, and, if you do so, how you will find your way into the kind of education that talks less about how various details should be dealt with and is concerned primarily with giving the teachers the means of gaining the intimate relationship to the child of which I have spoken.

To achieve this, something else is needed. When we receive a child into our school, we are expected to teach and train the youngster. We introduce all kinds of activities, such as writing, reading, and arithmetic, but really we are assaulting the child's nature. Suppose that we are to give reading lessons. If taught in the traditional way, they are certainly onesided, for we make no appeal to the child's whole being. Essentially, we are actually cultivating a malformation, even a predisposition toward illness. And, when teaching writing, we are cultivating a tendency toward illness in another direction. In teaching young children, we are making assaults on them all of the time, even if this is not always evident because the illness lies hidden and dormant. Nevertheless, we have to make continual attacks upon the children. At our stage of civilization there is no other way. But we must find ways and means of making amends for those continual assaults on our children's health. We must be clear that arithmetic represents a malformation, writing a second malformation, and reading a third malformation, not to speak of history or geography! There is no end to it and it leads us into a real quandary. To balance out those malformations, we must constantly provide what will make good the damage; we must harmonize what has been disturbed in the child. It is most important to be aware of the fact that, on one hand, we must teach children various subjects but that, on the other, we must ensure that, when we do so, we are not hurting them. The right method in education therefore asks: How do I heal the child from the attacks which I continually inflict? Awareness of this must be present in every right form of education.

But this awareness is possible only if we have insight into the whole human organization and really understand the conditions of that organization. We can be proper teachers and educators only if we can grasp the principle of the inflicting of malformations and their subsequent harmonization. For we can then face a child with the assurance that, whatever we are doing when teaching a subject and thereby attacking one or other organic system, we can always find ways and means of balancing the ill effects of leading the child into onesidedness.

This is one realistic principle and method in our education that teachers can use and that will make them into people who know and understand human nature. Teachers, if they are able to know the human being as a whole, including the inherent tendencies toward health and illness, can gradually develop this ability.

Here something arises that contemporary, more materialist medicine might well consider to lie outside its province. However, it immediately gains in importance as soon as we look at growing human beings from the point of view of predisposition toward illness, or—if I make this remark somewhat prematurely—of a predisposition toward health. For then it flows into our educational philosophy of the human being.

Today, health and illness are considered polar opposites: a person is either healthy or ill. But, if we go to the root of the matter, the actual situation is not that at all. Health and illness do not represent opposing poles, for the opposite of illness is something quite different from health. Everyone has a clear idea of illness. Naturally, it is only an abstract and general concept for, actually, we have to do only with particular cases of illness and ultimately, in fact, only with the individual who is ill. However, we could certainly gain an idea of what illness is if we started from the perspective of malformation and gradually reached a picture of how such malformations came about, at first less noticeably, in an animal or human organism. What occurs in the case of illness is that a single organ, or organic system, no longer operates within the overall general organization but assumes a separate role. This has a complement in the case of a single organ completely merging into the total organization.

Let us consider this in the light of Goethe's principle. Instead of a healthy leaf growing at a certain point, assume that a malformation occurs. But something else could also happen; namely, that the plant, instead of shooting into an individual organ, develops rather in the direction of the general, underlying tendency that really ought to remain in the spiritual sphere. In that case, the effect is that the single organ, instead of assuming its normal position within the organic whole, disperses its forces into the entire organism. The organ does not sufficiently predominate in the physical realm and consequently the whole thing becomes too spiritual, becomes too spiritualized, and the spiritual permeates the physical too strongly. This is a possibility. The situation, however, can also degenerate in a direction opposite to illness. The opposite polarity of illness consists in the single organ being sucked up, as it were, by the general organism. In human beings this is something that creates a feeling of well-being and sensual bliss. From this point of view, the opposite of illness is what we might call the ensuing overabundant bliss.

Consider the same thing from the perspective of language. If you form a verb from the adjective "sick," you get the verb "to sicken" [German *kranken* = to hurt someone's feelings]. If you take an adjective and a verb expressing the polar opposite [of *kranken*], you get "pleasant" and the verb, "to please". Between these two extremes—of feeling ill, or pained and the feeling of well-being or organic bliss—a healthy human being must hold the balance. That is what health really is: holding the balance.

This assumes special significance when we face a growing child. In what condition is the growing child whom we have to teach? Let us take a child who attends primary school; that is, between the change of teeth and puberty. What is the significance of the change of teeth?

I have already described its significance in one of the "academic courses" held here in Dornach:[2] namely, certain forces of growth saturate and form the child's organism until the second teeth appear. During the first seven years of childhood, the forces that are active in the child's organism, forming its physical body, behave in a way similar to latent heat when it changes into outwardly perceptible, liberated heat. I showed how what works into the human sphere of soul and spirit as an organizing principle in the physical body is transmuted into human soul and spirit in their own indigenous realm. Once the second teeth have developed, a child no longer needs the forces of growth that have been active previously in the inner organism. With the change of teeth, those forces are liberated, transformed into forces of soul and spirit, and find a healthy life through what we can do when we, as teachers, receive the child into our care.

To put it schematically, we may say that the young child's physical organism is imbued with a force that organizes it structurally. When the child sheds its milk teeth and reaches

2. "Hochschulkurse"—Academic Courses: October 1920 and April 1921 (Collected Works/GA 76).

school age, that force comes to a natural completion and what had been working previously in the child's physical organism becomes liberated and reappears metamorphosed in the realm of soul and spirit as forces of ideation, memory, and so on. Once teachers recognize that what they engage in primary education is "liberated soul forces"—comparable to liberated heat—they can begin to understand the inner relationship of soul and spirit with the bodily-physical nature in a new way. That is, for example, whereas these soul forces were previously occupied in the physical body, they are now at our disposal. We can use them to meet the educational demands of contemporary culture. For, after all, we cannot and must not ignore the cultural conditions of our time.

Hence, at this stage we approach the child knowing that, as we receive him or her into our school, something of a soul and spiritual nature is withdrawing from the physical sheaths. We know that a part of this organizing force gradually transforms itself into soul and spirit. And yet, to a certain extent, throughout this transition, this organizing force retains its previous manner of working in the physical body—for the part that is liberated is still accustomed to working in accordance with physical forms. We are not doing the child any good, therefore, if we teach it something totally alien to its nature. We do this, for example, if we begin by teaching the letters of the alphabet. These, in themselves, are alien to the child and, besides, have undergone many changes since the days of pictorial writing.

That is why, in the Waldorf school, we introduce writing on an entirely artistic basis. We do not teach children writing directly, but let them draw and paint fundamental forms so that, through those drawn forms, they can externalize what has been released during the change of teeth. When children move their hands and fingers in drawing and painting, we find that what was weaving in the soul realm is now projected into the whole human being in accordance with the form of the body. By our bringing the child's hands and fingers into movement in this way, what had been working previously in the soul realm as an organizing principle can continue its activity.

In this way, we become conscious of what we are really dealing with. We are dealing with the fact that, from birth to the change of teeth, a child's body is still deeply permeated by soul-spiritual forces that, later, free themselves from the physical. Once the soul-spiritual nature withdraws, the physical aspect develops more onesidedly. Indeed, as far as the physical aspect is concerned, we have here a process similar to those malformations in which the entire plant force shoots into a single organ. In the case of malformations, the result is simply a malformation.

In a human being, the normal course of events is that, at the time of the change of teeth, the physical body becomes separated from the soul-spiritual aspect. When the teeth change, therefore, we are actually dealing with the beginning of processes that, if they were allowed free development in a onesided way, would become processes of illness. This explains the cause of some illnesses that often accompany the change of teeth. We can now recognize their origin. It is possible to look into the child's organism with absolute clarity when the milk teeth are being shed. If one does so, one will see that, when the soul and physical natures separate, the physical body tends to become onesided and harden. One can see how the same forces are at work within their higher, normal limits. Should they proliferate, they would lead to processes of illness. In normal processes, there are always subtle ones present that can lead to illness if the separating tendencies are allowed free rein. We may therefore say that when a child acquires second teeth, it is at the threshold of illness. The more we as teachers engage the liberated forces of the child's soul and spirit—in anthroposophical terminology we call them *etheric forces*—the greater the healing effect. [3] This is so as long as the activities are suited to the child's physical nature. By teaching in an artistic way, we have to re-unite a child's soul and spirit harmoniously with its bodily-physical nature. We must be able to recognize the tendencies toward illness and health in the child's body, for we must make that body into a fit instrument for what is evolving in the child.

Let us now look at the other end of the primary school, at puberty. There, we find exactly the opposite situation. Whereas, during the second dentition, the soul-spiritual withdraws from the child's organism, becoming liberated from and abandoning the physical body, during puberty the soul-spiritual nature, which has meanwhile developed, longs to return to the physical body, to permeate and impregnate it. During puberty, there is a submerging of the soul-spiritual nature into the physical body. The body is being saturated and thoroughly permeated by the soul and spirit nature, which works instinctively. It is the reverse process, moving in the direction opposite to that of a state of illness; that is, it tends towards inner well-being and, we might say, a feeling of gratification. While teaching the child during the years of primary education, we must continually maintain a balance between what is striving toward the soul-spiritual becoming liberated at the beginning of the second dentition and what is instinctively streaming back from the soul-spiritual sphere into the physical body at puberty. The teacher must always strive toward equilibrium in the child during the coming and going that take place during the whole period between seven and fourteen.

---

3. On "etheric forces," see Rudolf Steiner, *Theosophy*, and Bockemühl et al. *Toward a Phenomenology of the Etheric World* (Spring Valley, New York: Anthroposophic Press, 1985).

This becomes a particularly important and absorbing task for the teacher between the child's ninth and tenth years. Because the two streams of forces meet at the half-way stage, the child is then in a condition in which it can develop in all possible directions. Much depends on whether the teacher, as the guide, says the right words to the child, choosing the right moment between the ninth and tenth years, or whether he or she misses this unique moment. Much of great significance for the child's entire life depends on whether the teacher knows how to meet this challenge between the ninth and tenth years.

Only if one understands the mutual interplay between soul and spirit and the physical body can one really understand the essence of childhood at this age and know how to deal with the child. One cannot talk about education at all without grasping these rising and falling processes, which are onesided only if we separate them into soul and spirit on one hand and bodily-physical on the other. In reality, they constantly interweave and interpenetrate. We understand the child rightly only if we can see this flowing together of soul-spiritual and bodily-physical as a single unified, coherent process.

What, then, is our task as teachers after the onset of the second dentition? We must continually make sure that the soul and spiritual forces that become liberated are employed in accordance with true human growth and development. In a way, we must "copy" the forces that want to leave the physical organism; we must copy them in the realm of the soul and the spirit in order that, by this means, they can find their right place in human growth and development. In other words, we must know the child and teach in a way that activates the inner harmony of the child's whole being. We must draw everything out of the child's inner nature.

As teachers, when pupils approach puberty, we must look for the essence of their being in their letting their soul-spiritual nature submerge into their physical nature. Indeed, our adolescents will develop abnormally if we do not recognize that we must fill their souls and spirits that are submerging into their physical being with an interest for the whole world. If we do not do this, they will become inwardly excitable, nervous, or neurasthenic (not to speak of other abnormalities). As teachers, we must direct our pupils' interests to the affairs of the wide world, so that our young people can take into their bodily being as much as possible of what links them to the outer world. When a child first enters school, we must know what is striving to be liberated so that we can work on it, but, at the stage of adolescence, we must become "people of the world" in order to know what can interest our adolescent students. By so doing, we can ensure a healthy descent of our teenagers' souls and spirits, which are about to become submerged in their physical bodies. That will prevent their becoming too strongly absorbed in the flesh and they therefore will not lose themselves narcissistically in pleasure. We should aim at helping them to become persons who live in the world and who are able to become free from too much self-interest. Otherwise, they will become trapped in egotism. We must help them toward a true and harmonious relationship with the world.

These are the kind of things that can show how a method of education arising from a consideration of the whole human being must proceed. Naturally, I could give only brief indications here. It can be quite painful to hear, in response to one's talking to educationalists and teachers—as happened to me recently—"How strange to hear that medical knowledge also happens to be a part of teaching." These medical aspects do not "happen" to belong to education; they are an absolutely essential ingredient. Without medical awareness, a healthy pedagogy is unthinkable, for it would become lost in empty abstractions, which are useless when one really has to deal with children.

We know the spirit only if we knows how it works into matter. Spiritual science therefore does not lead into a nebulous "cloud cuckoo-land" but to real insights into the material aspects of life. Those who seek to escape from matter will find no entry into the spirit, but those who recognize the power of the spirit and how it manifests in matter will. This is the only basis for a healthy theory and practice of education. If people would only see how anthroposophical spiritual science seeks to work everywhere in a realistic way and how it is remote from all unhealthy pursuits such as proliferate today in various kinds of mysticism, spiritualism and the like—if people would only recognize how real knowledge of the spirit is a reality and at the same time true knowledge of matter—then they would be able to judge the anthroposophical approach in a healthier manner. For, after all, and one must repeat it, natural science has celebrated its great triumphs in modern times; it has cultivated great and important results for human development. But such science, in reality, is like a study of the human body without a soul or a spirit. Just as the human body makes sense only if the soul is seen as part of it, so natural science is comprehensive only when it is complemented by a science of the spirit.

If one does not know very much about spiritual science, one might not be in a position either to accept or to criticize this statement. Yet, if a person studies specific "chapters" of this science, he or she will come to realize its mission more and more. Especially in the field of education we can see how spiritual science, arriving at universal concepts, gives teachers what they need in school with regard to knowledge of tendencies toward health and sickness. Spiritual science overcomes specialization, fragmentation, and gives teachers what they need to use knowledge of health and illness when they teach children at school. If a doctor had to stand beside the teacher, their cooperation could only be external. A healthy situation is possible only when teachers let their knowledge of health and illness permeate their entire teaching. Such a thing, however, is possible only if a living science, as striven for by anthroposophy, includes knowledge of healthy and sick human beings.

How often have I emphasized that anthroposophical spiritual science addresses itself to the whole human being! In anthroposophy, the whole human being enters into a relationship to what a specific branch of spiritual science can contribute. If teachers are introduced to both healthy and sick development of children in a living way, if they can harmonize those two aspects of child development, then their own feeling life will at once be motivated. They will face each individual child with his or her specific gifts as a whole human being. Even if teachers teach writing in an artistic way, they can still be guiding their children in a onesided way that comes very close to malformation. But, at the same time, they also stand there as whole human beings, who have a rapport with their children's whole beings and, in this capacity, as whole human beings, they themselves can be the counterforce to such onesidedness.

If, as a teacher who has a living relationship with everything that has to do with the human being, I *must* lead the child in a onesided way when I teach reading or writing, then I must go about it in such a way that, precisely through leading the child into onesidedness, I at the same time bring about an inner harmonization of the child's being. The teacher who always has to work toward the wholeness of all things must stand there as a whole person, whatever subject is taught. There are two things that must always be present in education. On one hand, the goal of each particular subject and, on the other, the 1,001 imponderables which work intimately between one human being and another. If teachers are steeped in knowledge of the human being and the world—and if their knowledge begins to live in them when they face their children—we have a situation similar to that of the plant. As the entire formative force shoots into a single organ in a plant, only to withdraw again in the right way and shoot into another organ, so the teacher holds this totality, this unifying force, in his or her own being, while guiding the child from stage to stage.

Spiritual science can stimulate this way of guiding the child, for spiritual science is related to all branches of outer, natural science in the same way as the soul is related to the human body. And, as, according to the old saying, a healthy soul is to be found in a healthy body, so, too, in and through a healthy science of nature there should be found a healthy science of the spirit, a healthy anthroposophy.

QUESTIONS AND ANSWERS

QUESTIONER I:
Gifted educators and teachers have an instinctive feeling for what needs to be done with a child upon reaching school age, both in and out of school. But it is not clear to me what the relationship of anthroposophically-based education is toward such instinctive responses to children. I would therefore like to ask whether such pedagogical instincts are frowned on in the Waldorf school or whether, in fact, they have their place within the framework of anthroposophical pedagogy.

QUESTIONER II:
I would like to ask how we are to understand children's illnesses as you have spoken of them. By "illness," do you mean a condition that orthodox medicine would call a state of illness, or an abnormality of the child's physical constitution, or perhaps ill humor, grumpiness, or similar disturbances?

RUDOLF STEINER:

Regarding the relationship between pedagogical instincts and what I said today, I would like to make the following observations. In general, the two approaches need not be considered contradictory, but one must be clear about the whole process of human evolution. The farther back we go in human evolution, the more consciousness decreases, until we come to what corresponds to the entirely instinctive mode of behavior of the animal world. The natural course of development in human evolution is a gradual lessening of instinctual life and a gradual supplementing of instinctive behavior by a healthy, conscious grasp of life's realities. We can see how important it is to bring about this transformation in the right way when we observe how, precisely in our times, previously healthy instincts have to a large extent fallen into disorder. For instance, while we can see quite clearly that children living in the country will grow up harmoniously even without a great deal of schooling, we can also see clearly that if we let city children depend on their instincts or—as has happened—if we seek to guide those instincts according to current pedagogical ideas, we can cause a great deal of harm. Unless, therefore, guided by our inner being, we are moved once more in a safe direction, we will not be able to foster wholesome and healthy conditions simply by calling abstractly for more instinctive ways of living—ways of living that in fact must today be replaced by powers of reasoning and intellect. Certainly, instinctive life still plays its part, but it is more and more on the wane.

To give a striking example, I can recall something that once happened in my presence. This is the kind of situation often encountered nowadays. It certainly took me by surprise. I was invited by a good friend whom, from earlier days of friendship, I knew to be quite a healthy eater—a person who also knew when to stop eating. Once, after an interval of several years, I was invited to his house again. And there, on the table, to my great surprise, I saw a pair of scales, complete with weights, on which he weighed every piece of food that he ate. This was surely clear evidence that, in his case at least, healthy instincts had greatly decreased!

Similar symptoms can also be observed in other life situations—for instance, if one studies the current curricula in our schools. We do not find in our schools the kind of teaching material that, if healthy instincts were working, would be found appropriate for, say, children in their eighth or ninth year. The curriculum is handled there according to quite different criteria—such as abstract rules regarding human and nonhuman matters. But curriculum—how we plan and work out our ways of education today—has a grave consequence for our children's health. We must find our way back to a concrete grasp of the interweaving of health-giving and illness-inducing tendencies in the human being. What I mean by health-giving or illness-inducing will become clear in a moment.

Words, such as "ill-humor" and "grumpiness" were mentioned in this regard. Such words land us immediately amid abstractions. This is certainly not what I mean, for we would then be judging a child's whole soul being abstractly. This is the very thing that a healthy, anthroposophically-based education must overcome. An anthroposophically-based education would make us realize, for example, that when a child suffers from mood disturbances, we are to watch for irregular glandular secretions. The glandular secretions are of far greater significance to us than the outer symptoms of ill humor, which will disappear when we tackle the problem at the source; that is, in the child's physical organism. What we must do is to look far more deeply into the whole relationship between the child's soul and spirit on one side and its physical and bodily existence on the other.

As educators dealing with children, teachers are naturally dealing only with inherent tendencies, with nascent states of unhealthy conditions. Teachers deal with subtle, rather than cruder, symptoms. And when such symptoms become pathological, they must be dealt with appropriately. I think it clear from what I have said that, in education, we deal with tendencies toward extremes and with finding ways and means of balancing them.

QUESTIONER:
We have heard that, during puberty, the adolescent is to be brought into contact with the affairs of the world and away from his or her individual spiritual self. What does this mean in concrete terms? What are the teachers supposed to do about it?

RUDOLF STEINER:
I did not say "away from his or her spiritual self." I weigh my words carefully and what I say surely has a clear meaning. I did not say "away from his or her spiritual self" but simply away from himself or herself; that is, adolescents must be prevented from pressing the spiritual element too strongly into their inner being and thereby experiencing a kind of inner pleasure. At the onset of puberty, we must try to awaken the students' interest for what is happening in the world. This is a fundamental objective in our curriculum for adolescents. We must awaken a particular interest in such subjects as geography and history—subjects that lead students away from themselves and out into the world. Adolescents need subjects that, because they are totally unconnected with any form of inner brooding, will counteract any too strong preoccupation that they might have with their inner life. It all depends on working out an appropriate curriculum in concrete detail.

RUDOLF STEINER:
(in answer to a further question): I have already indicated that teachers preparing their lessons should seek to work with their pupils' natural and healthy forces of organic growth. If we know how to study the healthy growth of the human organism, we also know that implicit in different physical forms is a constant inner striving toward movement. For instance, if we look at the human hand without preconceptions, we can see that its form really makes little sense in the state of rest. Each finger is living proof of the hand's inherent desire to move. And, conversely, such latent movement also seeks an appropriate form for the state of rest. This is an indication of something that is outwardly apparent. But such organismic tendencies can also be followed into the innermost organization of the human being. So that, if I am familiar with living anatomy, living physiology, then I also know what harmonizes with inner potentialities in the realm of movement.

From this point of view, it certainly does not correspond to the nature of children when a teacher makes a child scratch a copper-plate Gothic style letter "a" as is popular today. This is a form for which there is really no justification. There is no inner connection between the way the fingers want to move and the form of the letter that finally evolves after having gone through many intermediary stages.

During earlier phases of human evolution, quite different signs were painted to represent a form of writing which was still in harmony with the human organization. Today, the forms of our conventional letters no longer have any direct relation to the inner organization of human beings and that is why we must draw out of the child what is akin to its inner organization before introducing it to the present form of our alphabet. But, if you bring this to the attention of educational authorities, they become quite alarmed, wondering how on earth they are to know what the human organism is demanding, how they could possibly expect teaching to be done in an artistic style when pupils are aged six, and so on (this may be rather different in the case of practicing teachers who are often very open to these ideas because they can see new perspectives being opened up by them).

There is but one answer to all this—one must learn to do it! It is something that must be brought to the notice of anyone interested in education. It is not the task of anthroposophy to spread an abstract conception of the world that might satisfy people who like to rehash what they have heard, or who enjoy telling themselves what they must do for their own advancement. Anthroposophy is broadly based and has many ramifications that can lead us to the most intimate knowledge of human nature. One can truly say that anthroposophy offers an opportunity of fructifying the various sciences, especially in areas that, today, are not generally accessible to them.

And so we can say that we have to get to know the human being thoroughly so that, when we receive the child into primary education, we know from its whole organism how it should move its fingers and hands when learning to write, and also how it should learn to think.

The other day, I had the opportunity to take a visitor into a first grade writing and reading lesson. This subject can be taught in a hundred different ways. In the Waldorf school, teachers are given absolute freedom in their application of basic principles. Education is an altogether free art. The subjects might remain the same, but teachers may present their content in their own individual ways and according to the specific character of their pupils. People sometimes cannot see how these two aspects are related to each other.

How was this lesson given after the young pupils had been in the first grade for only a few months? A child was called out and told to run in a circle in a given number of steps. Immediately afterward, the teacher drew a circle on the blackboard to show how the movement experienced by the child while running looked when seen with the eyes.

Then, a second child was called out and asked to run in a much smaller circle inside the first circle, using only two steps. A third child had to run yet another circle, this time using three steps. All of the children were thoroughly involved in what was going on and they transposed what they had experienced with their whole being into what became visible on the blackboard. Their interest was directed not only to what the eye could see, but to what they experienced with their whole being. So there were three circles. When yet another one was run, the children noticed that, because of the size, the fourth circle intersected the smaller ones within the first large circle. And so it went on. This is how children were given the opportunity of gaining an experience out of their whole being that they could then transfer to the visual sphere. If, on the other hand, children are told to draw forms immediately, it is their heads that are mainly engaged—which amounts to a onesided occupation. Everything that pupils do at this stage should come out of their whole being, writing included.

But this does not mean that every teacher is now supposed to follow the same example! I merely gave an example here to show how one teacher undertook the task of applying underlying principles in the classroom. What I introduced in the Teacher Training Course, prior to the opening of the Waldorf school in Stuttgart, was not meant to be copied pedantically by teachers in their actual teaching. It was presented as living substance so that the school could become a living organism. As for rules and regulations, they can of course always be put together. If three people—or thirty, or perhaps only twelve—sit together in order to work out what, according to their lights, are the necessary conditions for creating a model school—committing to paper every rule in order of priority and with the appropriate paragraphs—they can of course produce wonderful schemes, even if they themselves are not graced with outstanding intelligence, even if they are only of ordinary or possibly even below average intelligence. The relevant points can be discussed in detail until impressive rules and regulations are finally agreed upon. But these are not likely to be of any use at all when it comes to the actual teaching. What always matters most is how things work out in practice.

QUESTIONER:
How should one proceed when educating a nervous child?

RUDOLF STEINER:
The expression "a nervous child" is extremely ambiguous. Thus, it is impossible to give definite directives. One must have a clear description of the child's symptoms and one needs to know the age of the child. In such a case, one really must be able to consider all the relevant factors within the general context. For instance, it might happen that one is shown a child, let us say, three or four years old, who is extremely fidgety and likely to romp about wildly. There are such children. They throw themselves to the ground and go into terrible tantrums. Their behavior is distinctly discomfiting for the parents who may thereby suffer a great deal of unhappiness. Then they ask what they could possibly do with such a child. Often, though by no means in every case, one would like to ask them to do nothing at all, for the worst thing in such a situation is to suppress the symptoms. Such a child simply has to get rid of an overabundance of energy so that, later on, it may develop normally—as one might put it. It is sometimes necessary to point out that it is better not to meddle with a child's development

by taking pedagogical measures. The important thing is to find out from the child's overall constitution what is or is not beneficial in each individual case. The same thing applies when one considers conditions of health or illness. How often does one hear these or similar remarks from persons with fixed ideas of what is normal, "If someone's pulse beat is irregular, one has to cure it by this or the other means." That might be perfectly correct in many instances but is by no means so in every case. Some people, due to their general constitution, actually need a slightly abnormal pulse! And so also in this case. One must know the overall constitution of a child before one can make definite statements. As always, anthroposophy aims to free people from living with abstract ideas. Such a question as "How should one deal with a nervous child?" is an abstraction. One is never confronted by a general situation, but always by a particular child who needs to be dealt with individually.

QUESTIONER:
How can anthroposophy give a lead with regard to pupils' finding their future careers?

RUDOLF STEINER:
I really do not know what is meant by this question! If I were to answer it in the abstract, I would have to say that an anthroposophical environment would in itself engender in a young person the right inclination to finding an appropriate vocation. In general, the choice of a career is dealt with far too schematically. As a rule such a choice is already linked to a person's destiny. People are sometimes insufficiently flexible—they believe that only a particular profession can bring them inner satisfaction. That might well be so in cases where professions have a markedly individualistic stamp, but to look for a lead to finding the right career in what anthroposophy has to

say on the subject sounds to me removed from the realities of life. I cannot really see the meaning of the question.

The chairman asked whether there were any further questions. There were none.

RUDOLF STEINER:
I hope that this talk, given in all brevity and presented as a mere outline of our broadly based but specific theme, has contributed something toward a better understanding of the aims of anthroposophy. These aims are never intended to be isolated from actual life situations. When the essence of anthroposophy is fully grasped, it will always lead into the realities of life, into life itself.

4

The Fundamentals of Waldorf Education

AARAU — NOVEMBER 11, 1921

When, after the collapse of Germany in 1918, a movement toward social renewal was born in Stuttgart with the aim of lifting the country out of the chaos of the times and guiding it toward a more hopeful future, one of the oldest friends of the anthroposophical movement, Emil Molt, conceived the idea of founding the Waldorf school in Stuttgart. Mr. Molt was in a position to implement that idea almost immediately, for he was in charge of an industrial enterprise employing a large number of workers. Thanks to the excellent relations existing between the management of that enterprise, the Waldorf-Astoria Cigarette Factory, and its workers, it proved possible to attract all of the workers' children to the school. In this way, more than two years ago, the Waldorf School was founded, primarily for working class children.

During the past two years, however, the school has grown almost from month to month. Today we have not only the original pupils of the Waldorf school—whose guidance was put into my care—but also many other children from all social classes and backgrounds. Indeed, the number of pupils who have found their way into the Waldorf school from all quarters of the population is now considerably larger than the original number of founding pupils, the children of the factory workers.

This fact shows the Waldorf school to be in practice a school for children of all types, coming from different classes and cultures, all of whom receive the same teaching, based on our own methods.

The idea of the Waldorf school grew out of the anthroposophical movement, a movement that, nowadays, attracts a great deal of hostility because it is widely misunderstood. In tonight's talk, and by way of introduction, I will mention only one such misunderstanding. This misunderstanding asserts that it is the aim of anthroposophy or spiritual science, particularly in its social aspects, to be revolutionary or somehow subversive, which is not at all the case. I must emphasize this because it is of special importance for our pedagogical theme. As anthroposophical spiritual science seeks to deepen and fructify the many branches of science that have developed in the cultural and spiritual sphere during the last three or four centuries, it has no intention whatever of opposing modern science in any way. Nor does it wish to introduce amateurism into modern science. It only wishes to deepen and to widen the achievements of modern science, including modern medicine.

Likewise, the education arising from anthroposophical spiritual science does not wish to oppose the tenets of recent educational theory as put forward by its great representatives. Nor does it wish to encourage amateurism in this field either. Acknowledging the achievements of modern natural science, anthroposophical spiritual science has every reason to appreciate the aims and the achievements of the great educators at the end of the nineteenth and the beginning of the twentieth centuries. Anthroposophy has no wish to oppose them. It wishes only to deepen their work by what can be gained through anthroposophical research. It wishes to stand entirely on the ground of modern pedagogical thinking. However, it does find it necessary to expand the scope of modern pedagogical thinking and I shall endeavor to give a few outlines of how this is to be done.

Though the Waldorf school takes its starting point from anthroposophical spiritual science, it is nevertheless not an ideological school—and this I hope will be accepted as an important fact. The Waldorf school is not in the least concerned with carrying into the school anthroposophical dogma or anthroposophical convictions. It seeks to be neither ideological nor sectarian nor denominational, for this would not be in character with anthroposophical spiritual science. Unfortunately, the opposite is often erroneously believed.

The Waldorf school, which has its roots in anthroposophy, is a school applying specific methods and classroom practices, as well as pedagogical ideas and impulses drawn from anthroposophically-oriented spiritual science. When we founded the school, we were simply not in a position to insist on such radical demands as are frequently made by some modern educators who maintain, for instance, that, if one wants to educate children properly, one has to open boarding schools or the like in the country, away from cities. There are many such endeavors today, and we have no objection to them on our part. From their point of view, we fully understand the reasoning behind their demands. In the Waldorf school, however, we are not in the same happy position. We had to accept a given situation. The possibility was granted to us to place what was to become the Waldorf school in a city, in the very life of a city. There was no question of first insisting on the right outer conditions for the school. What mattered was to achieve what had to be achieved through the principles and methods of our education under given circumstances.

It is a characteristic feature of anthroposophical spiritual science that it can adapt itself to any outer conditions, for it wants to be able to work under all conditions of life. It has no wish to chase after utopian ideals, but wants to create something in harmony with the human potential of its members out of the immediate practical conditions and the practical needs of life in any given situation.

To repeat, no dogma is to be carried into the school. What a person standing within the anthroposophical movement does gain, however, is a way of knowing that involves our whole humanity. The educational life of our times tends to favor a certain intellectualism. Therefore there is no need to fear that the Waldorf school teaches its pupils that a human being consists not only of a physical body (as you can read in many anthroposophical writings) but also of an etheric body, supplying the formative and organic growing forces at work in the physical body, and also of an astral body that, during earthly life, carries what was developed during pre-earthly existence—prior to physical birth or, rather, conception, and so on—into the human physical organization. None of this is taught in the school. But, if we know that human beings, when observed with scientific accuracy, consist of body, soul, and spirit, and if we grasp how this is revealed in the child as a human being in the making, we gain a deeper and truer knowledge of the human being than is possible through present-day natural science.

We do not grasp this deeper knowledge of human beings and all that anthroposophical spiritual science can learn about them only with our powers of thinking: the whole human being—thinking, feeling, and willing—is involved. This, however, is not the substance from which the training methods for work in the Waldorf school are to be drawn. Rather, anthroposophical knowledge creates in our teachers the forces of will to do all that they can for growing children in accordance with the demands of each child's organization. However paradoxical it might sound, the child is the teacher "par excellence" in the Waldorf school. For Waldorf teachers are fully convinced that what they meet in their children, week by week, year by year, is the outer manifestation of divine and spiritual beings who have come down to earth from a purely soul and spiritual existence in order to evolve in a physical body on earth between birth and death. They realize that each child's being unites—by means of the stream of heredity coming through the parents and their ancestors—with what is bestowed physically and etherically. Waldorf teachers have an enormously deep reverence for the young human being who, in the first days after birth, already shows how an inner soul-being manifests in physiognomy, in the first limb movements, and in the first babblings that gradually grow into human speech. Anthroposophical knowledge of human beings creates a deep reverence for what the divine world has sent down to earth and that inner attitude of reverence is the characteristic feature of Waldorf teachers as they enter their classrooms every morning. From the daily revelations of this mysterious spirit and soul existence, they discover what they as teachers must do with their children.

This is the reason why one cannot formulate the methods of the Waldorf school in a few abstract rules. One cannot say: point one, point two, point three, and so on. Rather, one has to say that, through anthroposophical spiritual science, a teacher comes to know the growing human being and learns to observe what looks out of a child's eyes and reveals itself in a child's fidgety leg movements. Because teachers are thoroughly grounded in an understanding of the whole human being, their knowledge of anthroposophy fills not only their intellect, with its capacity to systematize, but embraces the whole human being who also feels and wills. These teachers approach their pupils in such a way that their methods acquire a living existence that they can always modify and metamorphose, even in larger classes, to suit each individual child.

Anyone hearing all of this in the abstract, might well respond, "These crazy anthroposophists! They believe that a human being does not only have a physical body which, as a corpse, may be carefully examined and investigated in physiology and biology; they also believe that human beings have etheric, and even astral, bodies; and they believe that we can know these if we practice certain soul exercises; they believe that if we strengthen our thinking to the point where the whole human being is transformed into a kind of 'supersensible sense organ'—if I may use Goethe's expression—we can see more than we do in ordinary human life." It is easy to poke fun at such "crazy anthroposophists," who speak in these terms of supersensible beings in the sense-perceptible world. But if these convictions—based not on weird fantasies but on well-grounded knowledge—are carried into teaching, those whose task it is to educate the young are able to look upon growing children realistically as beings of body, soul, and spirit. And this is how children must be observed if our pupils' innermost being is to be revealed.

I do not wish to say anything derogatory about what, today, is referred to as experimental psychology or experimental pedagogy. I appreciate what those scientific disciplines are capable of achieving and I acknowledge it. But, just because of those disciplines, we must deepen our educational life all the more. For, aside from their positive aspects, they demonstrate that we are not getting closer to children in a direct and natural way, but that, on the contrary, we have become more estranged from them than ever before. External experiments are made with children to ascertain how their thinking, their memory, and even their will function. From the ensuing statistics, rules and regulations are then drawn up. Certainly, such findings have their uses, especially if one is an anthroposophist. But, if we regard them as the "be-all and end-all" and a foundation for education, we only adduce proof that, in actual fact, we have not reached the child's real being in any way. Why do we find it necessary to engage in experiments at all? Only because the direct, immediate relationship of teacher to child, which was there in ancient, Biblical times—if I may use this expression—has been lost under the influence of our modern materialistic culture. External experiments are made because there no longer exists a direct feeling and understanding for what actually happens within a child. The fact of these external experiments is in itself proof that we have lost a direct relationship with our children and that we should try to rediscover it with all available power.

When we study contemporary experimental psychology and pedagogy, it often seems as if the experimentalist were like someone observing a person riding a horse to see how he or she does on a smooth path as compared to more difficult terrain. From such observations, the experimentalist then compiles statistics: on the smooth path, such and such a distance in fifteen minutes; on a slippery path, so many miles; on an uneven path, so many more miles; and so on. This is the way of working that we also find, more or less, in experiments made to determine whether a child will remember something for a quarter of an hour, or whether a child omits so and so many of the words to be remembered, and so on. To return to our simile; if we were to compile statistical details about the rider, we would have to take into consideration not only the state of the paths but also what the horse was capable of doing on the particular paths observed, and so on. But we will never succeed by this method in discovering anything about the rider him- or herself (although it would of course be perfectly possible to include the rider in statistical observations as well). What really matters is not just that we carry out external experiments on those to be educated, but that, as teachers, we are in direct, natural contact with children through our understanding of their inner nature.

In anthroposophical spiritual science, one learns to know what is given when a baby is born. We learn that a child bears within itself not only what we can perceive with our senses but also a spirit-soul being that has united with the physical embryo. We learn to know exactly how this spirit-soul being develops, just as we learn from material science how the physical germ develops within the hereditary flow. We learn to recognize that, independent of the inherited traits, something of a supersensible spirit and soul nature enters. Without teaching it as a dogma—and I must emphasize this repeatedly—this perspective nevertheless becomes a means of orientation for the teacher—something that serves to guide a teacher's observations of children even before they enter school.

In the case of a child learning to speak, the following premise is useful. We must observe not only what belongs to the stream of heredity but also what develops in the child from spiritual depths. Language is part of this. When one observes human beings in the light of anthroposophical spiritual science—discriminating between the more inward, astral body and the more outward etheric body—one comes to know the nature of the human will in quite a new way. One sees the will as more allied to the astral body while thinking, for instance, is seen to be more closely connected with the etheric body. One learns to know how these members interact in speaking. For in observing and experiencing life, we have to do not only with outer facts but with placing these facts in the right light.

Let us now take a well trained observer of life, someone schooled in anthroposophy to know human beings, and place this person beside a child who is going through the process of learning to speak. If we have really learned to look into a child's soul life, recognizing the imponderables at play between adult and child, we can learn more about children's psychology by observing real-life situations than, for example, the eminent psychologist Wilhelm Preyer[1] did by means of statistical records. For instance, we learn to recognize the immense difference between, let us say, when we hear a mother or father speaking to a child to calm it down and saying, "Ee Ee," and when we hear someone who is speaking to a child about something more outward in its immediate environment and says, "Hsh, hsh!" With every vowel sound, we speak directly to a child's feeling life. We address ourselves to the innermost being of the child's soul. With the help of spiritual science, we learn to know how to stimulate a particular soul area. And in this way, we bring about a certain connection between adult and child that generates a close relationship between teacher and pupil, allowing something to flow from the teacher directly to the child's inmost feeling.

If, for example, we speak to a child about how cold it is outside, that child is taken into the realm of consonants (as in "Hsh-Hsh"), where we work directly on the child's will. We can thus observe that we stimulate in one instance a child's feeling life, and in another the child's life of movement, which lives in will impulses.

With this example, I merely wanted to indicate how light can be shed upon everything, even the most elementary things, provided we have a comprehensive knowledge of life. Today,

---

1. Wilhelm Preyer, 1841–1897, physiologist and psychologist, published the book, *The Soul of the Child*, Leipzig, 1881.

there exists a magnificent science of language from which education certainly can benefit a great deal. That science, however, studies language as if it were something quite separate from human beings. But, if we are schooled in anthroposophical spiritual science, we learn to look at language not as something floating above human beings who then take hold of it and bring it into their lives; we learn that language is directly connected with the whole human being, and we learn to use this knowledge in practical life. We learn how a child's inner relationship to the vowel element is connected with a warming glow in the feeling life, whereas the consonantal element—whatever a child experiences through consonants—is closely linked to the movements of the will.

The point is that one learns to observe the child more intimately. This kind of observation, this empathy with the child, has gradually been lost. So often today, when attempts are made to educate young human beings, it is as if we were actually circumventing the child's real being —as if our modern science of education had lost direct contact with the child to be educated.

We no longer recognize that speech is organically linked to all processes of growth and to all that happens in a child. Fundamentally, we no longer know that, in raising a child to become an imitator in the right way, we are helping it become inwardly warm and rich in feelings. Until the change of teeth, around the seventh year, children depend entirely on imitation and all upbringing and education during those early years depends basically upon this faculty. Only if we gain a clear understanding of this faculty of imitation during the first years of life and can follow it closely from year to year will the hidden depths of a child's inner nature be revealed to us, so that we can educate our pupils in ways that, later on, will place them fully into life.

This is true not only of speech but of whatever we must teach our children before they enter school. As I say, until the second dentition, a child is, fundamentally speaking, wholly dependent on imitation. Anthroposophical spiritual science allows us to study the young child's faculty of imitation in all spheres of life—and speech, too, develops entirely through imitation. But the study of the faculty of imitation enables us to look more deeply into the nature of the growing human being in other ways too. Although contemporary psychology constantly thinks around the problem of how the human soul or—as it is sometimes called—the human spirit is connected to the human physical body, it is not in a position to come to any exact idea of the relationship between the human soul and spirit on one side and the physical and bodily counterpart on the other. Basically, psychology only knows the physical aspects of the human being, when, like a corpse, the body is bereft of soul and spirit; on the other hand, it has distanced itself from the human soul and spirit as I have spoken of them. This situation can best be clarified with the help of a particular example. Contemporary science does not appreciate the importance of such phenomena as the second dentition occurring around the seventh year. But the kind of observation fostered by spiritual science reveals how a child's soul forces change during this process. A child's memory and ability to think, and also a child's faculty of feeling, become very different during these years. Actually, one cannot see a child's soul life develop before about the seventh year. But where was this emerging soul life with which we have to deal when the child enters school before the seventh year? Where was it previously?

The method employed by scientific thinking is perfectly appropriate in the inorganic realm. When physicists today study certain substances that emit heat after undergoing a particular process, they ascribe that heat to the warmth that was formerly contained within the substance as "latent" or hidden heat. Then they study how, when subjected to a particular process, that latent heat is liberated or released from the physical substance. They would not dream of concluding that the radiating heat had somehow come into the matter from outside, but they study the condition in which the heat existed while already present there. This way of thinking, inaugurated by physics, can be transferred to the more complicated realm of the human being.

If, from an anthroposophical point of view, we study how a child's memory and will assume a particular configuration in the seventh year, we will not conclude that these new faculties have suddenly "flown into the child." We will assume that they developed within the child itself. But where were they previously? They were active in the child's physical organism. In other words, what the teacher must educate was previously a latent, hidden force in the child's own being. That force has been liberated. As long as children need the forces that will culminate with the pushing out of the second teeth, those forces will be active in the child's inner realm. With the shedding of the milk teeth and the emergence of the second teeth, those forces—like the latent heat in certain substances—are released from their task and reveal themselves as new soul and spiritual capacities. These we then actively engage in our teaching.

Only by studying examples from real life can we learn to understand how soul and body work together. We can engage in endless philosophical speculation about the relationship of soul and body to each other but, when studying early childhood up to the seventh year, we must observe the actual facts. Only then will we recognize that forces that have left the organic bodily realm after the change of teeth are free to be used by the teacher in quite a new way.

The same principle applies to the whole span of human life. All of the speculative theories about the relationship of soul and body that we can find in books on philosophy and physiology are useless unless they are based on a mode of observation that is exact according to proper scientific methods.

If we observe such things further, we realize that the forces in a child with which we deal as teachers are the same that were previously engaged in building up the organism. We know, too, that those forces must now assume another form and that, if we are to teach children, we must come to know those forces in their new form. But we must also get to know them in their original form—since they must be used for learning, we must be able to recognize them in their original task. Well, a lot more could be said about this. I will only point out that it is because of those forces, working in the depths of the organism, creating life, that a child imitates up to the seventh year. To understand a preschool child, we must always bear in mind this faculty of imitation.

For example, parents complain that their son has stolen money. They are looking for advice. You ask how old the child is and are told that he is four or five years old. It might sound surprising, but a child of four or five does not really steal. Such a child is still at the stage of imitation. And so, if you ask further questions, you discover, for instance, that the child has seen his mother taking money out of a cupboard every day. The child imitates this action and, consequently, he too takes money. I have even known a case in which a child took money out of a cupboard but, instead of buying sweets, bought things to give to other children. There was nothing immoral in this behavior, only perhaps something somewhat amoral, something imitative.

An incident like this makes us realize that, in educating children, we are dealing with imponderables. As teachers, we must realize that, when we stand before a child who is an imitator, we must be mindful even of our thoughts. Not only our actions but our thoughts too must be of a kind that a child can safely imitate. The entire upbringing of preschool children must be based on this principle of imitation. Even if it might sound strange, awareness of this principle must lie at the foundation of a really healthy form of early education.

The forces that make a child an imitator to such an extent that it imitates even the slightest hand movement appear when the child is about seven as the liberated forces with which educators and teachers have to deal. Looking more closely at this development, one recognizes that, whereas a child is a compulsive imitator up to the age of seven, during the next seven years, up to puberty, the pupil needs to experience a natural sense of authority in the teacher as the right guide on life's path. The experience of authority becomes the main educational principle for children between the change of teeth and puberty—a principle that develops naturally to become the basic relationship between teacher and pupil.

It is all too easy to speak abstractly about this relationship based upon a natural sense of authority. If we wish to guide it in the right direction at every moment of our teaching life, we need anthroposophical knowledge of the human being.

Today, many people speak about the necessity and the importance of visual instruction, practical demonstration, and so forth—and they are in a certain sense quite right to do so. It is certainly right for some subjects. Anything that can be outwardly observed can be brought to the child by these methods. But we must consider, above all, the moral order of the world and human religious feelings—that is, everything pertaining to the spiritual nature of the world. The spiritual is imperceptible to outer senses and if we take the so-called visual instruction method too far, we lead children into believing in only what is sense perceptible—that is, into materialism. What really matters at this age is that through the natural relationship to the teacher, the child feels, "This adult, who is my guide, knows what is right and behaves in a way I long to emulate." (If I describe such a feeling as an adult, it is naturally quite different from how a child would experience it.)

During the first seven years, then, a child's activities mirror and imitate its surroundings—above all through gestures, including the subtle inner gestures that live in speech. But, during the next seven years, children develop under the influence of the words that come from the naturally accepted authority of their teacher. In order to appreciate the importance and value of this natural sense of authority, one must have a thorough foundation in true knowledge of the human being.

You would hardly expect someone like myself who, many years ago, wrote a book called *Intuitive Thinking as a Spiritual Path: A Philosophy of Freedom* to support a reactionary social belief in authority. So it is not on the basis of any authoritarian intention but solely on educational grounds that I maintain that the most essential principle, the most important force in education, between the age of seven and puberty, lies in a pupil's belief that the teacher, as an authority, knows what is right and does what is right. This must sink down into the child.

If students do not develop on the basis of this belief in the authority of the teacher, they will be unable, when older, to enter social life in a wholesome manner.

To understand this, we need only to know what it means for a child willingly to accept something on the basis of authority. I realize that this is for many people rather a controversial point but, actually, it is controversial only for those who, fundamentally speaking, lack the will to look at life in its entirety.

For instance, let us assume, say, that, in our second year of life nature did not dispose the form of our fingers so that they grow and develop—that nature made our fingers such that, as it were, they were cast in hard stereotyped forms. What would we do then! Insofar as we are human, then, we are growing, continuously changing beings. And as educators, likewise, this is the kind of essence that we must pour into children's souls. We must not impose on our children anything that creates sharply contoured pictures, impressions, or will impulses in them. Just as our fingers do not retain the contours that they had when we were two but rather grow on their own, so all ideas, thoughts, and feelings that we pour into children during their school years must have the essence of growth in them.

We must be quite clear: what we bring to an eight-year-old cannot be clear-cut or sharply contoured. Rather, it must have an inner capacity for growth. By the time the person is forty, it will have become something quite different. We must be able to see the *whole* human being. Anyone who does not appreciate the principle of authority during these years of childhood has never experienced what it really means when, for instance, in the course of one's thirty-fifth year, out of the dark recesses of memory, one understands some concept of history or geography—or some concept of life—that one accepted without understanding at the age of nine on the authority of a well loved teacher or parent, having taken it simply on faith. When such a concept emerges in the soul and is understood with the mature understanding of several decades later, this becomes an animating principle that calls up an indefinable feeling that need not be brought to full consciousness: something from one's earliest years lives on in one's soul. It is in this sense that we must be able to follow the forces of growth in nature.

Our educational principles and methods must not be tied up in fixed formulae. Rather, they must become a kind of refined, practical instinct for action in those who educate from a living knowledge of human beings. Teachers will then find the right way of dealing with children rather than merely artificially grafting something onto the souls in their care. This is not to deny what has been promulgated by the great pedagogues of the nineteenth and early twentieth centuries. On the contrary, it is actually applying it in the right way.

Those who wish to become Waldorf teachers know quite well that they cannot join the school as amateurs, as dilettantes. They must be moved by all that nineteenth- and twentieth-century education has brought forth. But, at the same time, they must also bring to the Waldorf school the living insight into human beings of which I have spoken. Here one feels prompted to quote Goethe's dictum, "Consider well the *what*, but consider more the *how*." You will find excellent expositions of the *what*—with regard to foundations and principles—in theoretical texts on education. Even quite idealistic thoughts are sometimes expressed there, but all of this represents only the *what*. The point is not to formulate abstract principles but to be able to apply them in a living way, with inner soul warmth.

I am fully convinced that if a group of people were to sit together—they need not even be outstandingly clever—to draft the blueprint for an ideal school, their schemes, put into order of priorities—first, second, third, and so forth—would be quite excellent. They would be so convincing that one could not improve on them. It is quite possible to think out the grandest ideals and turn them into slogans for great movements of reform and so on. But, in life as it is, all of this is of little value. What matters is to truly observe life, to bear in mind the living human being who is capable of doing what needs to be done under given circumstances. "Consider well the *what*, but consider more the *how*."

And so, what matters is that love of the child lies at the root of all of our educational endeavors, and that all teaching be done out of an inner, living experience. Against this background, the foundations of our education become quite other than they usually are. With this in mind, then, I would like to put into words a fundamental underlying principle, once more in the form of an example.

A child is supposed to form an inner picture of a definite concept. It is capable of doing so but, in our attempts to communicate something abstract—something of an ethical and religious nature—we can proceed in different ways. For example, let us imagine that the teacher wants to convey to pupils—naturally in accordance with the children's age and maturity—the idea of the immortality of the human soul. We can do this with a comparison. There are two ways in which we can do this. One would be as follows. As teachers, we can believe that we are terribly clever, whereas the child is still young and terribly ignorant. On this basis, we could invent a comparison and say, "Look at the chrysalis. The butterfly comes out of the chrysalis." Then, after describing this process pictorially, we might say, "Just as the butterfly emerges from its chrysalis, so the human soul, when a person passes through the portal of death, leaves the body and flies into the spiritual world." This is one way of approaching the problem. Feeling greatly superior to the child, we think out a simile or comparison. But, if this is our underlying attitude, we will not be very successful. Indeed, this is a situation where imponderables play their part. For a teacher who has been schooled in anthroposophical spiritual science about the nature of the world and knows that there is spirit in all matter will not proceed from a feeling of being far more clever than the child. Consequently, he or she will not invent something for the child's benefit. That is to say in this case the teacher will firmly believe that what on a higher level represents the human soul leaving the body at death is represented in the natural order on a lower level by the emergence of the butterfly from the chrysalis. The teacher will believe in the truth of this picture. To this teacher, the image is a sacred revelation. These are two entirely different approaches. If I speak to the child out of a sacred conviction, I touch the child's innermost being in an imponderable way. I call forth in the child a living feeling, a living concept. This approach is generally true. We must neither underestimate nor overestimate what modern science has to say out of its exclusive interest in the external world.

Allow me to quote a somewhat far-fetched example to consolidate what I have been saying. As you know, there has been a great deal of talk about so-called "counting horses." Those horses perform quite special feats. I myself have not seen the *Elberfeld* horses, but I did see Herr von Osten's horse and witnessed how this horse, when questioned, stamped out the answers to simple arithmetical questions with one of its hooves. The horse stamped the correct number of times—one, two, three, four, five, six, and so on. In order to explain such a phenomenon and avoid falling into nebulous mysticism or mere rationalism, we need a certain ability to observe. Now, among the spectators of the counting horses was a certain private tutor in psychology and physiology who, having seen Herr von Osten's horse performing its tricks, declared that the horse stamped when a specific number was called out because it was able to detect very subtle and refined expressions in Herr von Osten's face. He claimed that when his master moved his face in a certain way after asking, "What are three times three?" the horse stopped stamping after nine stamps. Naturally, this learned gentleman had to prove that such looks or movements really existed in Herr von Osten's face. But this he was unable to do. In his learned dissertation, he stated, "These looks are so subtle and infinitesimal that a human being cannot detect them, and even I myself" —he added—"am unable to say anything about them." You see that all of his cleverness amounted to admitting his own lack of being able to discover the facial expressions that the horse was supposed to follow. In other words, the horse was more perceptive than this learned lecturer! A less biased spectator would have noticed that, while the horse stamped answers to arithmetical questions, Herr von Osten continually fed his horse with sugar lumps which he took from his rather capacious coat pocket. While apparently performing calculations, the horse was constantly relishing the sweet taste of the sugar lumps. I must ask you not to misunderstand me if I say that this way of treating the horse gave rise to a very specific form of a loving and intimate relationship, an inner relationship, and that this is really what was the root-cause of what was happening.

If one wants to discover this true relationship existing below the level of ordinary observation, one must begin with what the effect of such "love" can be. If one wants to understand such things properly, it is no good talking of hypnotism or suggestion in a general way, but one must understand the nature of such a subtle relationship. Neither nebulous mysticism nor mere rationalism will lead to one's solving the mystery, but only a knowledge of the human, and in this case also the animal, soul.

This is what matters above all if we wish to found a living method of education, as distinct from one based on mere principles and intellectual theories. This living method of education then guides us to observe the child from year to year. It is this *How*, this individual treatment of each child even within a larger class, that matters. It is possible to achieve it.

The Waldorf school has already demonstrated this fact during the first few years of its existence.

Here I can only give broad outlines, which can be supplemented by more detailed examples. First of all, we receive the child into our first grade, where it is supposed to learn writing and reading, perhaps also the beginnings of arithmetic and so on. Let us first discuss reading. Reading in our present culture is really quite alien to a young child. If we go back to ancient times, we find that a kind of picture writing existed in which each letter word still retained a pictorial connection with the object it represented. In our present system of writing or printing, there is nothing to link the child's soul to what is written. For this reason, we should not begin by immediately teaching children writing when they enter primary school in their sixth or seventh year. In the Waldorf school, all teaching—and this includes writing, which we introduce before reading—appeals directly to a child's innate artistic sense. Right from the start, we give our young pupils the opportunity of working artistically with colors, not only with dry crayons but also with watercolors. In this simple way, we give the child something from which the forms of the letters can be developed. Such things have been done elsewhere, of course. But it is again a matter of *how.* The main thing is that we allow the child to be active without in any way engaging the forces of the intellect but by primarily activating the will. On the basis of drawing and painting, we gradually lead a child's first will activities in writing toward a more intellectual understanding of what is written. We lead our children, step by step, developing everything in harmony with their own inherent natures. Even down to the arrangement of the curriculum, everything that we do at school must be adapted to the child's evolving nature. But, for this, anthroposophical knowledge of human beings is necessary.

I would here like to point out how one can observe the harm done to children when one does not give them concepts and feelings capable of growth, but makes them aware of the difference between the outer material world of fixed forms and their own inner mobile soul life at too early an age. Until about the ninth year, a child does not yet clearly discriminate between him- or herself and the outer world. One must be careful not to believe in abstract concepts, as some people do today who say, "Well, of course, if a young child bumps into the corner of a table, it smacks the table because it thinks that the table is also a living thing." This, of course, is nonsense. The child does not think that the table is a living object. It treats the table as if it were a child, too, simply because it cannot yet distinguish its own self from the table. Whether the table lives or not is beside the point. The child, as yet, has no such concept. We must always deal with realities, not with what we ourselves imagine intellectually. Until the ninth year, whatever we introduce to a child must be treated as if it had purely human qualities. It must be based on the assumption that the children's relationship to the world is such that every thing is a part of them—as if it were a part of their own organism. One can, of course, point to certain obvious examples where a child will differentiate between something in the external world and its own being. But, between the seventh and ninth years, we cannot further the finer aspects of education unless we bring to life whatever we teach the child, unless we make everything into a parable, not in a dead, but a truly living form. Everything must be taught in mobile and colorful pictures, not in dead static concepts.

Between the ninth and tenth years, a most important, significant moment occurs: it is only then that children really become conscious of the difference between their inner selves and their surroundings. This is the age when we can first intellectually introduce children to the life of plants and animals, both of whom have an existence apart from human beings. Something truly profound is taking place in a child's mind and soul at this time—a little earlier in the case of some children, a little later in others. Something is happening—fundamental changes are occurring—in the depths of their young souls; namely, they are learning to distinguish their inner selves from the outer world in a feeling way, but not yet by means of concepts. Therefore if teachers are aware of the right moment, and can find the appropriate words, they can—acting as the situation demands—do something of lasting value and importance for the whole life of these children aged between nine and ten. On the other hand, if they miss this significant moment, they can create an inner barrenness of soul or spiritual aridity in later life, and an attitude of everlasting doubt and inner dissatisfaction. But, if teachers are sufficiently alert to catch such a significant moment and if, by immersing themselves in the child's being, they have the necessary empathy and know how to speak the right words and how to conduct themselves rightly, they can perform an immense service for their children, who will derive benefit for the rest of their lives. In Waldorf education, the observation of such key moments in the lives of children is considered to be of utmost importance.

After this special moment in the ninth-tenth year, while all subjects had previously to be "humanized," teachers can begin to introduce simple descriptions of plants and animals in a more objective style. Then, between the eleventh and twelfth years, they can begin to introduce inorganic subjects, such as the study of minerals and physics. Certainly the lifeless world should be approached only after children have been fully immersed in the living world.

Thus the child is led—I mention only a few characteristic

examples—to the age when school normally comes to an end, to the age of puberty.[2]

How many countless discussions and arguments are going on these days about puberty from a psychoanalytical and from a psychological point of view! The main thing is to recognize that one is dealing here with the end of a characteristic life period—just as second dentition represented the end of an earlier period of development. Puberty in itself is only a link in an entire chain of metamorphoses embracing the whole of human life. What happened in the child at second dentition is that inner soul forces became liberated that had previously been working within the organism. Between the seventh and approximately fourteenth years, we try to guide the child in the ways I just described. With the onset of puberty, however, children enter the time of life when they can form their own judgments on matters concerning the world at large. Whereas, when younger, our children drew their inner being from the depths of their organism, as adolescents they now become capable of understanding the spiritual nature of the outer world as such. How to educate our children between their seventh and fourteenth years so that they are naturally guided to acquire an independent and individual relationship to the world—of which sexual life is only one expression—presents one of the greatest challenges to teachers. This is one of the most important problems of a truly living education. The sexual love of one person for another is only one aspect, one part of the whole fabric of human social life.

We must lead our adolescents to the point where they develop the inner maturity necessary to follow outer events in the world with caring interest. Otherwise, they will pass them by unheeded. As teachers, we must aim at turning our young

2. In 1921, the school-leaving age in Germany was fourteen.

human beings into social beings by the time of puberty. We must also try to cultivate in them religious feelings, not in a bigoted or sectarian way, but in the sense that they acquire the seriousness necessary to recognize that the physical world is everywhere permeated by spirit. They should not feel inwardly satisfied with merely observing the outer sense world but should be able to perceive the spiritual foundations of the world everywhere.

During prepubescence, when pupils open their inner being to us, believing in our authority, we must be what amounts to the whole world for them. If they find a world in us as their teachers, then they receive the right preparation to become reverent, social people in the world. We release them from our authority, which gave them a world, into the wide world itself.

Here, in only a few words, I touch on one of the most important problems of cognition. If we train children to make their own judgments too early, we expose them to forces of death instead of giving them forces of life. Only teachers whose natural authority awakens the belief that what they say and do is the right thing, and who in the eyes of the child become representatives of the world, will prepare their pupils to grow into really living human beings when, later on, they enter life. Such teachers prepare their pupils not by controlling their intellect or their capacity to form judgments but by setting the right example as living human beings. Life can evolve only with life. We make our students into proper citizens of the world by presenting the world to them in a human being—the teacher—not through abstract intellectual concepts.

I can characterize all of this in a few sentences, but what I am suggesting presupposes an ability to follow in detail how growing children evolve from day to day. By the power of his or her example, the way in which a teacher carries something through the door into the classroom already helps a child to develop further toward finding its own way in life. If we know this, we need not make amateurish statements, such as that all learning should be fun. Many people say this today. Try to see how far you get with such an abstract principle! In many respects learning cannot bring only joy to the child. The right way is to educate children by bringing enough life into the various subjects that they retain a curiosity for knowledge, even if it does not reward them immediately with pleasure. How a teacher proceeds should be a preparation for what pupils must learn from them.

This leads quite naturally to cultivation of the pupils' sense of duty. We touch here upon a sphere that extends far beyond what belongs to the field of education. We touch on something where a method and practice of education based on spiritual foundations directly fructifies the whole of cultural life.

We all of us surely look up to Schiller and Goethe as leading spirits. To have studied and written about them for more than forty years, as I have, leaves one in no doubt as to one's full, warm appreciation of their work and gifts. There is, however, just one point that I would like to make in this context.

When, in the 1790s, Schiller, having distanced himself from Goethe for all kinds of personal reasons renewed an intimate friendship with him, he wrote his famous—and sadly too little appreciated—*Letters on the Aesthetic Education of Man*. Schiller wrote these letters under the influence of how Goethe worked, thought, and viewed the world. In those letters, which are about aesthetic education, we find a strange sentence: "Only when we play are we fully human, and we play only when we are human in the truest sense of the word." With that sentence, Schiller wanted to point out how ordinary life essentially chains us into a kind of slavery, how the average person, forced to live under the yoke of necessity, suffers under the burden of outer life. In general, people are free to follow their own impulses only when engaged in artistic activities, when creating and enjoying art, or when behaving like children at play, acting only in accordance with their own impulses. What Schiller describes in his aesthetic letters is a beautiful and genuine conception of what it is to be human.

On the other hand, the letters show that with the advance of our modern scientific, technological civilization and for the sake of human dignity, exceptional persons like Schiller and Goethe found it necessary to demand that human beings should be allowed freedom from the daily round of duties. To become fully human, people should be relieved of the coercion of work so that they can be free to play. If we bear in mind the social conditions imposed on us by the twentieth century, we realize that we have completely changed our attitude toward life. Realizing that everyone must accept the demands of life, we feel that we carry an intolerable burden of responsibility upon our shoulders.

We must learn how to make life worthwhile again, from both the social and individual points of view, not only by introducing more play but by taking up our tasks in a more human way. This is the reason why the social question is today first of all a question of education. We must teach young people to work in the right way. The concept of duty must be brought into school, not by preaching, but in the right and natural way—which can be achieved only through a thorough, well grounded, and correct knowledge of human nature.

If we do so, we shall be founding schools for work, not schools following the attitude that teaching and learning are merely be a kind of "playing about." In our school, where authority plays its proper part, pupils are expected not to shy away from the most demanding tasks. In Waldorf schools, students are encouraged to tackle whole heartedly whatever is to be mastered. They are not to be allowed to do whatever they feel like doing.

It is with this in view that the Waldorf school has been founded. Children are to learn to work in the right way; they are to be introduced to life in the world in the full human sense. This demands work for social reasons and also that, as human beings, the students should learn to face one another and, above all, themselves in the right way. For this reason, apart from conventional gymnastics, which originally evolved from human physiology and hence has its values, we have also introduced eurythmy[3]—a new art of movement, cultivating body, soul and spirit; a visible form of language and music—into the Waldorf school.

You can find out more about eurythmy in Dornach. Just as there are speech and music that you can hear, so there also is a kind of language and music that uses the medium of gestures and movements evolved from the organization of the human body, but not as is done in dance or mime. It can be performed by groups of people who express in this new way the kind of content that is usually expressed through audible speech and music. Since its introduction in the Waldorf school some two years ago, we have already been able to observe that pupils from the lowest to the highest grades take to eurythmy lessons with the same natural ease with which little children take to speaking, provided that the lessons are given properly, in a way suited to each age group.

---

3. See, for instance, Rudolf Steiner, *An Introduction to Eurythmy* (Hudson, New York: Anthroposophic Press, 1984) and Marjorie Spock, *Eurythmy* (Spring Valley, New York: Anthroposophic Press, 1980).

Once, during an introductory talk before a eurythmy performance in Dornach, I spoke about eurythmy to an audience that happened to include one of the most famous physiologists of our times (you would be surprised if you heard his name). After saying that we had no wish to denigrate the value of gym in schools, but that the time would come when such matters would be judged with less prejudice and that eurythmy, with its movements involving a person's soul and spirit, would then come into its own, the famous physiologist approached me and said, "You said that gymnastics has its own beneficial value in modern education and that it is based on human physiology. As a physiologist, I consider gymnastics to be sheer barbarism!" It was not I who expressed this view, it was one of the best-known physiologists of our times!

Such an incident can lead us to appreciate the saying: "Consider well the *what*, but consider more the *how*." There are occasions when, reading books on educational theory and applied teaching, one feels like shouting for joy. *What* the great educationalists have achieved! But what matters is the right *how*. One has to find ways and means of implementing the ideas into practical life in the right way.

Every Waldorf teacher must seek this anew each day, for anything that is alive must be founded on life. Spiritual science eventually leads each one of us to an understanding of fundamental truths that, although they are always the same, nevertheless inspire us ever anew. Regarding our ordinary knowledge based on material things, we depend on our memory. What has been absorbed is remembered, to be recalled later from the store of memory. What we have once learned, we possess; it is closely linked to us. In everyday life, we certainly need our store of memory. Our intellect depends on memory, but living processes do not need memory—not even on the lower levels of our existence. Just imagine for a moment that you thought that what you ate once as a small child sufficed for the rest of your life. You have to eat anew every day because eating is a part of a living process and what has been taken up by the organism must be thoroughly digested and transformed. Spiritual substance likewise must be taken up in a living way and an educational method based on anthroposophy must work out of this living process.

This is what I wanted to describe to you in brief outline, merely indicating here what has been described in further detail in anthroposophical books, particularly those dealing with education. I wanted to draw your attention to the educational principles of the Waldorf school, a pioneering school founded by our friend Emil Molt, a school that has no desire to rebel against contemporary education. It seeks only to put into practice what has often been suggested theoretically. Anyone who surveys the kind of life which humanity, particularly in Europe, lives today will recognize the need to deepen many aspects of life. During the second decade of this twentieth century, following the terrible catastrophe that destroyed most of what was best in humanity, one must admit the importance of giving the coming generations soul-spiritual and physical-bodily qualities different from those received by our contemporaries who have had to pay so dearly in human life. Those who, as parents, must care for the well-being of their sons and daughters and who, most of all, have the right to see how education relates to life, will view our efforts without prejudice. Those among them who, as parents, have experienced the great catastrophes of our times, will doubtlessly welcome every attempt that, based on deeper social and spiritual awareness, promises the coming generations something better than what has been offered to many at the present time. The people who have most reason to hope for an improvement of conditions prevailing in contemporary education are the parents and they, above all, have the right to expect and demand something better from the teachers. This was the thinking and the ideal that inspired us when we tried to lay the educational foundations of the Waldorf school.

FROM THE DISCUSSION

QUESTIONER:
Dr. Steiner has spoken to us about the importance of authority in education, but this is something with which our young people want nothing to do. Every teacher, not to mention every priest, experiences it. Various currents run through our younger generation and one can certainly notice an aloofness on their part toward anything connected with the question of authority, be the authority in the parental home or authority regarding spiritual matters. Parents sometimes have the feeling that they no longer have any say in anything and that one must simply let these young people go their own way. On the other hand, one sometimes also witnesses the disillusionment of such an attitude and it is then painful to see young people not finding what they were seeking. There is something in the air that simply seems to forbid a respectful attitude toward older people, something that is like a deep-seated sting, ever ready to strike against authority in whatever form. Perhaps Dr. Steiner would be kind enough to tell us something about the reasons for this strange ferment among the younger generation. Why are they not happy? Why do they take special pleasure in complaining? It saddens us that we are no longer able to reach them. I have sought help by studying books dealing with this problem, but I have so far not found a single one that could

show me the way forward. I would therefore be very happy if Dr. Steiner could say something to give us insight into the soul of a young person.

RUDOLF STEINER:
This is, of course, a subject that, unfortunately, were I were to deal with it in any depth, would require a whole lecture of at least the same length as the one I have just given you—I say unfortunately because you would have to listen to me for such a long time! I would, however, like to say at least a few words in response to the previous speaker's remarks.

During my life, which by now can no longer be described as short, I have tried to follow up various life situations related to this question. On one hand, I have really experienced what it means to hear, in one's childhood, a great deal of talk about a highly esteemed and respected relative whom one had not yet met in person. I have known what it is to become thoroughly familiar with the reverence toward such a person that is shared by all members of the household, by one's parents as well as by others connected with one's upbringing. I have experienced what it means to be led for the first time to the room of such a person, to hold the door handle in my hand, feeling full of awe and reverence. To have undergone such an experience is of lasting importance for the whole of one's life. There can be no genuine feeling for freedom, consistent with human dignity, that does not have its roots in the experience of reverence and veneration such as one can feel deeply in one's childhood days.

On the other hand, I have also witnessed something rather different. In Berlin, I made the acquaintance of a well-known woman socialist, who often made public speeches. One day I read, in an otherwise quite respectable newspaper, an article of hers entitled, "The Revolution of our Children." In it, in true socialist style, she developed the theme of how, after the older generation had fought—or at least talked about—the revolution, it was now the children's turn to act. It was not even clear whether children of preschool age were to be included in that revolution. This is a different example of how the question of authority has been dealt with during the last decades.

As a third example, I would like to quote a proposal, made in all seriousness by an educationalist who recommended that a special book be kept at school in which at the end of each week—it may have been at the end of each month—the pupils were to enter what they thought about their teachers. The idea behind this proposal was to prepare them for a time in the near future when teachers would no longer give report "marks" to their pupils but pupils would give grades to their teachers.

None of these examples can be judged rightly unless they are seen against the background of life as a whole. This will perhaps appear paradoxical to you, but I do believe that this whole question can be answered only within a wider context. As a consequence of our otherwise magnificent scientific and technical culture—which, in keeping with its own character, is bound to foster the intellect—the human soul has gradually become less and less permeated by living spirit. Today, when people imagine what the spirit is like, they usually reach only concepts and ideas about it. Those are only mental images of something vaguely spiritual. This, at any rate, is how the most influential philosophers of our time speak about the spiritual worlds as they elaborate their conceptual theories of education. This "conceptuality" is, of course, the very thing that anthroposophical spiritual science seeks to overcome. Spiritual science does not want its adherents merely to talk about the spirit or to bring it down into concepts and ideas; it wants human beings to imbue themselves with living spirit. If this actually happens to people, they very soon begin to realize that we have gradually lost touch with the living spirit. They recognize that it is essential that we find our way back to the living spirit. So-called intellectually enlightened people in particular have lost the inner experience of living spirit. At best, they turn into agnostics, who maintain that natural science can reach only a certain level of knowledge and that that level represents the ultimate limit of what can in fact be known. The fact that the real struggle for knowledge only begins at this point, and that it leads to a living experience of the spiritual world—of this, generally speaking, our educated society has very little awareness.

And what was the result, or rather what was the cause, of our having lost the spirit in our spoken words? Today, you will find that what you read in innumerable articles and books basically consists of words spilling more or less automatically from the human soul. If one is open-minded and conversant with the current situation, one often needs to read no more than the first few lines or pages of an article or book in order to know what the author is thinking about the various points in question. The rest follows almost automatically out of the words themselves. Once the spirit has gone out of life, the result is an empty phrase-bound, cliché-ridden language, and this is what so often happens in today's cultural life. When people speak about cultural or spiritual matters or when they wish to participate in the cultural spiritual sphere of life, it is often no longer the living spirit that speaks through their being. It is clichés that dominate their language. This is true not only of how individuals express themselves. We find it above all in our "glorious" state education. Only think for a moment of how little of real substance is to be found in one or another political party that offers the most persuasive slogans or "party-phrases." People become intoxicated by these clichés. Slogans might to some degree satisfy the intellect, but party phrases will not grasp real life. And so it must be said that what we find when we reach the heights of agnosticism—which has already penetrated deeply into our society—is richly saturated with empty phrases. Living so closely with such clichés, we no longer feel a need for what is truly living in language. Words no longer rise from profound enough depths of the human soul. Change will occur only if we permeate ourselves with the spirit once more. Two weeks ago, I wrote an article for *The Goetheanum* under the heading, "Spiritual Life Is Buried Alive."[4] In it, I drew attention to the sublime quality of the writing that can still be found among authors who wrote around the middle of the nineteenth century. Only very few people are aware of this. I showed several people some of these books that looked as if they had been read almost continually for about a decade, after which they seemed to have been consigned to dust. Full of surprise, they asked me, "Where did you find those books?" I explained that I am in the habit, now and then, of poring over old books in second-hand bookshops. In those bookshops, I consult the appropriate catalogs and ask for certain chosen books to be delivered to wherever I am staying. In that way I manage to find totally forgotten books of all kinds, books that will never be reprinted but that give clear evidence of how the spirit has been "buried alive" in our times, at least to a certain extent.

Natural science is protected from falling into such clichés simply because of its close ties to experimentation and observation. When making experiments, one is dealing with actual spiritual facts that have their place in the general ordering of natural laws. But, excepting science, we have been gradually

---

4. See: Collected articles, 1923–1925 (in the Collected Works of Rudolf Steiner /GA36).

sliding into a life heavily influenced by clichés and phrases, by-products of the overspecialization of the scientific, technological development of our times. Apart from many other unhappy circumstances of our age, it is to living in such a phrase-ridden, clichéd language that we must attribute the problem raised by the previous speaker. For a child's relationship to an adult is an altogether imponderable one. The phrase might well flourish in adult conversations, and particularly so in party-political meetings, but if one speaks to children in mere phrases, clichés, they cannot make anything of them. And what happens when we speak in clichés—no matter whether the subject is religious, scientific, or unconventionally open-minded? The child's soul does not receive the necessary sustenance, for empty phrases cannot offer proper nourishment to the soul. This, in turn, lets loose the lower instincts. You can see it happening in the social life of Eastern Europe, where, through Leninism and Trotskyism, an attempt was made to establish the rule of the phrase. This, of course, can never work creatively and in Soviet Russia, therefore, the worst instincts have risen from the lower regions. For the same reason, instincts have risen up and come to the fore in our own younger generation. Such instincts are not even unhealthy in every respect, but they show that the older generation has been unable to endow language with the necessary soul qualities. Basically, the problems presented by our young are consequences of problems within the adult world; at least when regarded in a certain light, they are parents' problems. When meeting the young, we create all too easily an impression of being frightfully clever, making them feel frightfully stupid, whereas those who are able to learn from children are mostly the wisest people. If one does not approach the young with empty phrases, one meets them in a totally different way. The relationship between the younger generation and the adult world reflects our not having given it sufficient warmth of soul. This has contributed to their present character. That we must not blame everything that has gone wrong entirely on the younger generation becomes clearly evident, dear friends, by their response to what is being done for our young people in the Waldorf school, even during the short time of its existence.

As you have seen already, Waldorf education is primarily a question of finding the right teachers. I must confess that whenever I come to Stuttgart to visit and assist in the guidance of the Waldorf school—which unfortunately happens only seldom—I ask the same question in each class, naturally within the appropriate context and avoiding any possible tedium, "Children, do you love your teachers?" You should hear and witness the enthusiasm with which they call out in chorus, "Yes!" This call to the teachers to engender love within their pupils is all part of the question of how the older generation should relate to the young. In this context, it seems appropriate to mention that we decided from the beginning to open a complete primary school, comprising all eight classes in order to cover the entire age range of an elementary school.[5] And sometimes, when entering the school building, one could feel quite alarmed at the apparent lack of discipline, especially during break times. Those who jump to judgment too quickly said, "You see what a free Waldorf school is like! The pupils lose all sense of discipline." What they did not realize was that the pupils who had come to us from other schools had been brought up under so-called "iron discipline." Actually, they have already calmed down considerably but, when they first arrived under the influence of their previous "iron discipline," they were real scamps. The only ones who

5. Six to fourteen.

were moderately well-behaved were the first graders who had come directly from their parental homes—and even then, this was not always the case. Nevertheless, whenever I visit the Waldorf school, I notice a distinct improvement in discipline. And now, after a little more than two years of existence, one can see a great change. Our pupils certainly won't turn into "apple-polishers" but they know that, if something goes wrong, they can always approach their teachers and trust them to enter into the matter sympathetically. This makes the pupils ready to confide. They may be noisy and full of boisterous energy—they certainly are not inhibited—but they are changing, and what can be expected in matters of discipline is gradually evolving. What I called in my lecture a natural sense of authority is also steadily growing.

For example, it is truly reassuring to hear the following report. A pupil entered the Waldorf school. He was already fourteen years old and was therefore placed into our top class. When he arrived, he was a thoroughly discontented boy who had lost all faith in his previous school. Obviously, a new school cannot offer a panacea to such a boy in the first few days. The Waldorf school must be viewed as a whole—if you were to cut a small piece from a painting, you could hardly give a sound judgment on the whole painting. There are people, for instance, who believe that they know all about the Waldorf school after having visited it for only one or two days. This is nonsense. One cannot become fully acquainted with the methods of anthroposophy merely by sampling a few of them. One must experience the spirit pervading the whole work. And so it was for the disgruntled boy who entered our school so late in the day. Naturally, what he encountered there during the first few days could hardly give him the inner peace and satisfaction for which he was hoping. After some time, however, he approached his history teacher, who had made a deep impression on him. The boy wanted to speak with this teacher, to whom he felt he could open his heart and tell of his troubles. This conversation brought about a complete change in the boy. Such a thing is only possible through the inner sense of authority of which I have spoken. These things become clear when this matter-of-fact authority has arisen by virtue of the quality of the teachers and their teaching. I don't think that I am being premature in saying that the young people who are now passing through the Waldorf school are hardly likely to exhibit the spirit of non-cooperation with the older generation of which the previous speaker spoke. It is really up to the teachers to play their parts in directing the negative aspects of the "storm and stress" fermenting in our youth into the right channels.

In the Waldorf school, we hold regular teacher meetings that differ substantially from those in other schools. During those meetings, each child is considered in turn and is discussed from a psychological point of view. All of us have learned a very great deal during these two years of practicing Waldorf pedagogy. This way of educating the young has truly grown into one organic whole.

We would not have been able to found our Waldorf school if we had not been prepared to make certain compromises. Right at the beginning, I drafted a memorandum that was sent to the education authorities. In it, we pledged to bring our pupils in their ninth year up to the generally accepted standards of learning, thus enabling them to enter another school if they so desired. The same generally accepted levels of achievement were to be reached in their twelfth and again in their fourteenth year. But, regarding our methods of teaching, we requested full freedom for the intervening years. This does constitute a compromise, but one must work within the given situation. It gave us the possibility of putting into practice what we considered to be essential for a healthy and right way of teaching. As an example, consider the case of school reports. From my childhood reports I recall certain phrases, such as "almost praiseworthy," "hardly satisfactory" and so on. But I never succeeded in discovering the wisdom behind my teachers' distinction of a "hardly satisfactory" from an "almost satisfactory" mark. You must bear with me, but this is exactly how it was. In the Waldorf school, instead of such stereotyped phrases or numerical marks, we write reports in which teachers express in their own style how each pupil has fared during the year. Our reports do not contain abstract remarks that must seem like mere empty phrases to the child. For, if something makes no sense, it is a mere phrase. As each child gradually grows up into life, the teachers write in their school reports what each pupil needs to know about him- or herself. Each report thus contains its own individual message, representing a kind of biography of the pupil's life at school during the previous school year. Furthermore, we end our reports with a little verse, specially composed for each child, epitomizing the year's progress. Naturally, writing this kind of report demands a great deal of time. But the child receives a kind of mirror of itself. So far, I have not come across a single student who did not show genuine interest in his or her report, even if it contained some real home truths. Especially the aptly chosen verse at the end is something that can become of real educational value to the child. One must make use of all means possible to call forth in the children the feeling that their guides and educators have taken the task of writing these reports very seriously, and that they have done so not in a onesided manner, but from a direct and genuine interest in their charges. A great deal depends on our freeing ourselves from the cliché-ridden cultivation of the phrase so characteristic of our times, and on our showing the right kind of understanding for the younger generation. I am well aware that this is also connected with psychological predispositions of a more national character, and to gain mastery over these is an even more difficult task.

It might surprise you to hear that in none of the various anthroposophical conferences that we have held during the past few months was there any lack of younger members. They were always there and I never minced my words when speaking to them. But they soon realized that I was not addressing them with clichés or empty phrases. Even if they heard something very different from what they had expected, they could feel that what I said came straight from the heart, as all words of real value do. During our last conference in Stuttgart in particular, a number of young persons representing the youth movement were again present and, after a conversation with them lasting some one-and-a-half or two hours, it was unanimously decided to actually found an anthroposophical youth group, and this despite the fact that young people do not usually value anything even vaguely connected with authority, for they believe that everything has to grow from within, out of themselves, a principle that they were certainly not prepared to abandon.

What really matters is how the adults meet the young, how they approach them. From experience—many times confirmed—I can only point out that this whole question of the younger generation is often a question of the older generation. As such, it can perhaps be best answered by looking a little less at the younger generation and looking a little more deeply into ourselves.

A PERSON FROM THE AUDIENCE:

Perhaps, at this point, a member of the younger generation might be allowed to speak up. Please forgive my speaking plainly, but the truth is that we younger people have lost all respect for authority, for older people. Why? because our parents, too, have lost it. When talking to them or to other adults, we find that all that they can do is to criticize all kinds of unimportant, niggling things in others—thus showing their own generation in a bad light. We young people sometimes feel that those who are trying to educate us have become walking compromises, incapable of making up their minds on which side they stand, unable to state from the fullness of their hearts what their opinions are, unable to stand up for what they believe in. And we all the time have the feeling that our parents and educators do not in fact want to learn what we young are really like. Instead, they keep criticizing and condemning us. I need only to think of how we in our youth circle work together and what kind of things we study. For instance, we have read and discussed together Blüchner and Morgenstern. Just imagine those two polar opposites! This sort of thing happens with us all the time. Events in the world buffet us and nowhere can we find a center to give us a firm grasp. Nowhere can we find a really living person who can stand above it all with a comprehensive viewpoint—not even a person who can do so conceptually. How is it possible to teach unless behind everything that is taught there is a real living human being, whom one can feel coming through his or her teaching? . . . If that were to happen, it would rouse our enthusiasm. But, as long as our teachers do not approach us as human beings, as long as they are afraid even, sometimes, to laugh at themselves, we simply cannot feel the necessary confidence in them. I can say with complete conviction that we young people are really seeking adults to whom we can look up as authorities. We are looking for a center, for a firm grip with which we can pull ourselves up and that would enable us to grow into the kind of life that has an inner reality. That is why we throw ourselves into everything new that appears on the horizon: we always hope to discover something that could have a real meaning for us. But whenever this happens, we find nothing but a confusion of opinions and attitudes. We find judgments that are not real judgments at all, but are at best only criticisms.

If I may say something to the first speaker, who asked for a book to explain why young people behave as they do, I say: Don't read a book. To find an answer, read us young people! If you want to talk to the younger generation, you must approach them as living human beings. You must be ready to open yourself to them. Young people will then do the same and young and old will become clear about what each is looking for.

QUESTIONER:
As a teacher, I would like to ask Dr. Steiner whether he himself does not believe what the first speaker in today's discussion brought up; namely, that a quite new mood and spirit are stirring among young people today. This might perhaps be more evident in the larger cities, where even teachers with a deeply human attitude are no longer able to cope with difficulties as they were able to some fifty years ago. The source of the problem has been rightly sought in the older generation. Nevertheless, it cannot be denied that today's youth, under the influence of social-democratic ideas, is pervaded by skepticism to the extent that a teacher of Dr. Steiner's persuasion might not be able to imagine the kind of insolence and arrogance with which we have to put up. Socialistic contradictions are rife among the young, creating a false urge for independence in them that makes the teachers' tasks far more difficult than they were some time ago. Indeed, our job is now often almost impossible. What Dr. Steiner said gave the impression that the behavior of our youth merely reflects the shortcomings of their teachers. Certainly, teachers must take their share of the blame, but is it

all the teachers' fault? Are all teachers to blame? That is the question. Is it not the case that the few good teachers, who are not to blame, nevertheless bluntly state that a new and different kind of youth has appeared and that lack of faith and skepticism among them makes the teacher's task far more difficult?

RUDOLF STEINER:
Well, if you put the question in this way, it is impossible to move forward. Putting it thus will not produce anything fruitful. It is the wrong way to begin. To declare that young people have changed and that it might have been easier to deal with them fifty years ago is not the point at all; the crux of the matter is to find ways and means of coping with the problem. After all, the younger generation is there, growing up in our midst. Nor is it productive to speak of our youth as being led into skepticism by social-democratic prejudices. That is as futile as if one were to criticize something in nature because it was growing in an undesirable way—and that is what is happening with the young. They are growing up among us like products of nature. Rather than stating the fact that the young have changed, and that perhaps it was easier to deal with them fifty years ago, the only way forward is to find ways and means of enabling the older generation to cooperate with the young again. We shall find no answer if we merely point out that today's youth is different from what it was fifty years ago, as if this were something to be accepted more or less fatalistically. That kind of attitude will never lead us to find an answer to this problem. Of course, the young have changed! And, if we observe life, we can see that the change has its positive aspects, too—that we could speak of it as a change toward something greater. Let me remind you, for instance, of the generational conflicts that we find expressed in literature. You can read them or see them performed on the stage. You still sometimes

come across performances of plays from the late 1880s when the relationship between the younger and older generation was vividly portrayed. You will see that what we are discussing is an age-old problem. It has been regarded for centuries as a kind of catastrophe. By comparison, what is happening today is mere child's play! But, as I said before, merely to state facts will not lead us further.

The question everywhere is how to regain the lost respect for authority in individual human beings that will enable you as teachers and educators to find the right relationship to the young. That it is generally correct to state that young people do not find the necessary conditions for such a respect and sense of authority in the older generation and that they find among its members an attitude of compromise is in itself, in my opinion, no evidence against what I have said. This striving for compromise can be found on a much wider scale even in world events, so that the question of how to regain respect for human authority and dignity could be extended to a worldwide level. I would like to add that—of course—I realize that there exist good and devoted teachers as described by the last speaker. But the pupils usually behave differently when taught by those good teachers. If one discriminates, one can observe that the young respond quite differently in their company.

We must not let ourselves be led into an attitude of complaining and doubting by judgments that are too strongly colored by our own hypotheses, but must be clear that ultimately the way in which the younger generation behaves is, in general, conditioned by the older generation. My observations were not meant to imply that teachers were to be held solely responsible for the faults of the young. At this point, I feel rather tempted to point to how lack of respect for authority is revealed in its worst light when we look at some of the events of recent history. Only remember certain moments during the last, catastrophic war. There was a need to replace older, leading personalities. What kind of person was chosen? In France, Clemenceau, in Germany, Hertling—all old men of the most ancient kind who carried a certain authority only because they had once been important personalities. But they were no longer the kind of person who could take his or her stance from a direct grasp of the then current situation. And what is happening now? Only recently the prime ministers of three leading countries found their positions seriously jeopardized. Yet all three are still in office, simply because no other candidate could be found who carried sufficient weight of authority! That was the only reason for their survival as prime ministers. And so we find that, in important world happenings, too, a general sense of authority has been undermined, even in leading figures. You can hardly blame the younger generation for that! But these symptoms have a shattering effect on the young who witness them.

We really have to tackle this whole question at a deeper level and, above all, in a more positive light. We must be clear that, instead of complaining about the ways in which the young confront their elders, we should be thinking of how we can improve our own attitude toward young. To continue telling them how wrong they are and that it is no longer possible to cooperate with them can never lead to progress. In order to work toward a more fruitful future, we must look for what the spiritual cultural sphere, and life in general, can offer to help us regain respect and trust in the older generation. Those who know the young know that they are only too happy when they can have faith in their elders again. This is really true. Their skepticism ceases as soon as they can find something of real value, something in which they can believe. Generally speaking, we cannot yet say that life is ruled by what is right. But, if we offer our youth something true, they will feel attracted to it. If we no longer believe this to be the case, if all that we do is moan and groan about youth's failings, then we shall achieve nothing at all.

5

Educational Methods Based on Anthroposophy

CHRISTIANIA (OSLO) — NOVEMBER 23, 1921

PART I

First, I would like to thank the Vice Chancellor of this University, and you yourselves, ladies and gentlemen, for your friendly welcome. I hope that I can make myself understood, despite my inability to speak your language. Indeed, I apologize for my lack in that respect.

The theme that I shall present tonight and tomorrow night is the educational principles and methods based on anthroposophy. And so, here, right at the beginning, I must ask you not to look on the aims of anthroposophy as wishing to be in any way subversive or revolutionary— with respect either to scientific matters or any of the other many aspects of life where anthroposophy seeks to be productive.

On the contrary, anthroposophy seeks only to deepen and develop what has already been prepared by the recent spiritual culture of humanity. However, because of anthroposophy's deepened insight into human life and knowledge of the universe, it necessarily looks for a corresponding deepening and insight in contemporary scientific thinking. Likewise, it also looks for different ways of working practically in life—different from more accustomed and conventional ways.

Because of this, anthroposophy has found itself opposed by representatives of the spirit of the day. But it does not want to become involved in hostilities of this kind, nor does it wish to engage in controversy. Rather, it aims to guide the fundamental achievements of modern civilization toward a fruitful goal.

This is the case, above all, in the field of education. Apart from my small publication, *The Education of the Child from the Viewpoint of Spiritual Science*, published several years ago, I had no particular reason to publish a more detailed account of our educational views until, with the help of Emil Molt, the Waldorf school in Stuttgart was founded.[1]

With the founding of the Waldorf school, anthroposophy's contribution to the field of education entered the public domain. The Free Waldorf school itself is the outcome of longings that made themselves felt in many different parts of Central Europe after the end of the last, catastrophic war.

One of the many topics discussed during that time was the realization that perhaps the most important of all social questions was about education. And, prompted by purely practical considerations, Emil Molt founded the Free Waldorf school, originally for the children of the employees of his Waldorf Astoria Factory. At first, therefore, we only had children whose parents were directly connected with Molt's factory. During the last two years, however, children from different backgrounds have also entered the school. Hence, the Waldorf school in Stuttgart today educates children from a wide range of backgrounds and classes. All of these children can benefit from an education based on anthroposophy. In education, above all, anthroposophy does not wish to introduce revolutionary ideas, but seeks only to extend and supplement already existing achievements. To appreciate those, one need only draw attention to the contribution of

1. See note 16, lecture 1.

the great educators of the nineteenth and early twentieth centuries. Anyone with education at heart can feel only enthusiasm for their comprehensive ideas and powerful principles.

Yet, despite all of this, there remain urgent problems in our present education. As a result, not a year passes in which a longing for the renewal of education does not make itself felt in society.

Why should it be that, on one hand, we can be enthusiastic about the convincing educational ideas expressed by the great educators of our times, while, on the other, we experience a certain disenchantment and dissatisfaction in how education is carried out?

Let me give just one example. Pestalozzi has become world famous.[2] He certainly belongs among the great educators of our time. Nevertheless, thinkers of Herbert Spencer's caliber[3] have pointed out in the strongest terms that, although one might be in full agreement with Pestalozzi's educational principles, one cannot help realizing that the great expectations raised by them have not been fulfilled with their practical application. Decades ago, Spencer already concluded that despite Pestalozzi's sound and even excellent pedagogical ideas, we are unable at present to apply his general principles in practical classroom situations. I wish to repeat, ladies and gentlemen, that it is not new ideas that anthroposophy wants to introduce. Anthroposophy is mainly concerned with actual teaching practice.

Just as the Waldorf school in Stuttgart grew out of the immediate needs of a given life situation, what exists today as anthroposophical pedagogy and the anthroposophical method

---

2. Johann Heinrich Pestalozzi (1746–1827), Swiss educator.
3. Herbert Spencer (1820–1903), English philosopher. See his work *Education* [1861].

of education is not a product of theories or abstract principles but grows out of the need to deal practically with human affairs. Anthroposophy feels confident of being able to offer specific contributions for solution of human problems, particularly in the realm of education. What, then, are the fundamentals of this anthroposophy?

Anthroposophy has frequently drawn hostility and opposition, not because of an understanding of what it seeks to accomplish for the world, but rather because of misconceptions regarding it. Those within anthroposophy fully understand such hostility. For, on the basis of natural science and the cultural achievements of our times, modern humanity generally believes itself to have found a unified conception of the world. Anthroposophy then steps in with a call to our contemporaries to think about themselves and the world in an apparently quite different way. The contradiction, however, is only apparent. But people think initially that the insights provided by anthroposophy cannot be reconciled with the claims made by natural science.

Today, the human physical and bodily constitution is being thoroughly studied, on solid grounds, following the admirable and exact methods of modern natural science. And, as far as the human soul is concerned, its existence is no longer generally denied. On the contrary, the number of those who deny the existence of the soul and speak of "human psychology without a soul," as many did for a time, has already dwindled. Yet the soul itself is only observed by means of research into its physical aspects and by guesswork done on the basis of physical manifestations. Under such conditions, it is impossible to derive an educational practice, even with the best of theories and premises.

Thus, Herbert Spencer profoundly regrets the lack of a proper psychology for modern educational principles. But a true child psychology cannot possibly grow from the modern natural-scientific view of life. Anthroposophy, on the other had, believes that it is able to offer the basis for a true psychology, for real care of the human soul. However, it is a psychology, a care of the soul, that admittedly requires an approach very different from that of other contemporary psychological investigations.

It is all too easy to poke fun at anthroposophists who speak of other supersensible bodies, or sheaths, in addition to the physical body. It is often said that anthroposophy, when it speaks of the etheric body, which I also call the "body of formative forces," has invented or built up some strange fantasy, vision, or illusion. What anthroposophy says, however, is simply that a human being possesses not only a sense-perceptible, physical body (that can be examined according to established medical practice and whose underlying natural laws can be grasped by our intellectual capacity to systematize manifold phenomena) but also an *etheric* body, or a body of formative forces, that is of a more refined nature than the physical body and—apart from the etheric body—a still higher and more refined member of the human being, called the *astral* body. In anthroposophy, furthermore, we also speak of a very special aspect of the human being, which is summarized only by each individual's own self-awareness and is expressed by the word *"I."*

At first, there seems to be little justification for speaking of these higher aspects of the human being. By way of introduction, however, I would like to show how in actual and practical life situations—which are the basis of our educational views—anthroposophy speaks about, for example, the *human etheric body.*

This etheric body is not a nebulous cloud that is somehow membered into the physical body and perhaps extends a little beyond it here and there. Initially, of course, it is possible to imagine it like this but in reality it appears quite differently to anyone using anthroposophical methods of observation. The etheric body, in fact, is primarily a kind of regulatory agency and points to something that belongs, not so much to the human spatial organization, but to something of the nature of a "time organism."

When we study the human physical body, according to present day natural-scientific methods, we know that we can do so by studying its various organic parts—such as the liver, the stomach, or the heart—as separate entities. But we can also study those same organs from the viewpoint of their various functions and interrelationships within the whole human organism. We cannot understand certain areas of the human brain, for example, without knowing how they affect other organs, such as the liver, the stomach, and so on, effects that are instrumental in regulating the nourishment of those organs. We thus look upon the spatial, physical organism as having its own specific interrelationships. We see the physical organism as something in which single members affect each other in definite and determined ways.

Anthroposophy sees what it calls the human etheric body in the same way. It assigns to it an existence in time, but not in space as in the case of the physical body. What we call the human etheric body manifests itself at birth or, rather, conception and continues to develop through life until the point of death.

Disregarding the fact that a person can die before his or her natural life span has been reached, let us for the moment consider the normal course of a human life—in which case we may say that the etheric body continues its development through old age until the moment of death.

In what develops in this way, anthroposophical investigation sees an organic wholeness. Indeed, as the human spatial body is composed of various members—such as the head as the carrier of the brain, the chest organs as carriers of speech and breathing, and so on—so what manifests as the human etheric organization is likewise composed of various life periods, one following the other in the flow of time. We thus distinguish between the various component parts of the etheric body—which, as already stated, must be observed as existing in time and as consisting of spatially separated parts—by first considering the period from approximately a child's birth to its change of teeth. We can see an important part of the etheric body in this life period, just as we can see the head or the lungs in the physical body. Thereafter, we see its second member lasting from the second dentition until puberty and, though less clearly differentiated, we can also distinguish further life periods during the subsequent course of life. Thus, for instance, at the twentieth year, a completely new quality in a person's psychic and physical life begins to manifest. But, just as, for example, the cause of certain headaches can be traced to malfunctioning of the stomach or the liver, so can certain processes undergone in one's twenties or even during later life be traced back to definite happenings during the time between birth and the change of teeth. Just as it is possible to see processes of digestion affecting processes occurring in the brain, so is it possible to see the effects of what happened during a child's first seven years of life up, to the second dentition, expressed in the latest period of adult life.

When studying psychology, we generally find that only the present situation of a person's soul life is observed. Characteristics of a child's capacity of comprehension, memory, and so on are observed. Without wishing to neglect those aspects, students of anthroposophy must also ask themselves the following kind of question. If a child becomes subject to certain influences, say in the ninth year, how does that affect the deeper regions of his or her etheric psychic life and in what form will it re-emerge later on? I would like to illustrate this in more detail by giving you a practical example.

By means of our pedagogical approach, we can convey to a child still at a tender age a feeling of reverence and respect for what is sublime in the world. We can enhance that feeling into a religious mood through which a child can learn how to pray. I am purposely choosing a somewhat radical example of a moral nature. Thus, let us suppose that we guide a child so that it can let such a mood of soul flow into a sincere prayer. This mood will take possession of the child, entering the deeper regions of its consciousness. And, if we observe not only the present state of a person's soul life but his or her whole psychic constitution as it develops up to the moment of death, we will find that what came into existence through the reverence felt by the praying child goes "underground" to be transmuted in the depths of the soul. At a certain point, perhaps not before the person's thirties or forties, what was present in the devotional attitude of a praying child resurfaces as a power of blessing, emanating from the words spoken by such a person—especially when he or she addresses children.

In this way, we can study the whole human being in relation to his or her soul development. As we relate the physical to the spatial—for example, the stomach to the head—so can we relate and study through the course of a life what the power of prayer might have planted in a child, perhaps in the eighth or ninth year. We may see it re-emerge in older age as the power to bless, as a force of blessing, particularly when meeting the young. One could put this into the following words—unless one has learned to pray in childhood in a true and honest manner, one cannot spread an air of blessing in one's forties or fifties.

I have purposely chosen this somewhat radical example and those among you who are not of a religious disposition will have to take it more in its formal meaning. Namely, what I wanted to point out was that, according to anthroposophical pedagogy, it is not just the present situation of a child's soul life that must be considered; rather, the entire course of a human life must be included in one's considerations. How such an attitude affects one's pedagogical work will become plainly visible. Whatever a teacher or educator might be planning or preparing regarding any educational activity, there will always be the question in mind, what will be the consequences in later life of what I am doing now with the child? Such an attitude will stimulate an organic, that is, a living pedagogy.

It is so easy to feel tempted to teach children clearly defined and sharply contoured concepts representing strict and fixed definitions. If one does so, it is as if one were putting a young child's arms or legs, which are destined to continue their growth freely until a certain age, into rigid fetters. Apart from looking after a child's other physical needs, we must also ensure that its limbs grow naturally, unconstricted, especially while it is still at the growing stage. Similarly, we must plant into a child's soul only concepts, ideas, feelings, and will impulses that, because they are not fixed into sharp and final contours, are capable of further development. Rigid concepts would have the effect of fettering a child's soul life instead of allowing it to evolve freely and flexibly. Only by avoiding rigidity can we hope that what we plant into a child's heart will emerge during later life in the right way.

What, then, are the essentials of an anthroposophically based education? They have to do with real insight into human nature. This is something that has become almost impossible on the basis of contemporary natural science and the scientific conception of the world. In saying this, I do not wish to imply any disregard for the achievements of psychology and pedagogy. These sciences are the necessary outcome of the spirit of our times. Within certain limits, they have their blessings.

Anthroposophy has no wish to become embroiled in controversy here either. It seeks only to further the benefits that these sciences have created. On the other hand, we must also ask what the longing for scientific experimentation with children means. What does one seek to discover through experiments in children's powers of comprehension, receptivity to sense impressions, memory, and even will? All of this shows only that, in our present civilization, the direct and elementary relationship of one soul to another has been weakened. For we resort today increasingly to external physical experimentation rather than to a natural and immediate rapport with the child, as was the case in earlier times. To counterbalance such experimental studies, we must create new awareness and knowledge of the child's soul. This must be the basis of a healthy pedagogy. But, to do so, we must become thoroughly familiar with what I have already said about the course of an individual's life. This means that we must have a clear perception of the first life period, which begins at birth or conception, and reaches a certain conclusion when the child exchanges its milk teeth.

To anyone with an unbiased sense of observation, a child appears completely changed at the time of the change of teeth—the child appears different, another being. Only if we can observe such a phenomenon, however, can we reach a real knowledge of human beings.

Our understanding of the higher principles of the world has not kept pace with what natural science demands of our understanding of the lower principles. I need only remind you of what science says about "latent heat." This is heat contained by a physical substance without being outwardly detectable. But, when such a substance is subjected to certain outer conditions, the heat radiates outward, emitting what is then called "liberated heat." Science today speaks of forces and interrelationships of substances in the inorganic realm, but scientists do not yet dare to use such exact methods to deal with phenomena in the human realm. Consequently, what is said of body, soul, and spirit remains abstract and leaves those three aspects of the human being standing beside one another, as it were, with no real interconnection. We can observe the child growing up until the change of teeth and, if we do so without preconceptions, we can detect how, just after this event, the child's memory assumes a different character; how certain faculties and abilities of thinking begin to manifest; how memory works through more sharply delineated concepts, and so on. We can observe that the inner soul condition of the child undergoes a definite change after the second dentition. But what exactly happened in the child?

Today, I can only point in certain directions. Further details can be found with the help of natural science. When observing a child growing up from the earliest stage until the second teeth appear, one can discern the gradual manifestation of an inner quality, emerging from the depths and surfacing in the outer organization. One can see above all how, during those years, the head system develops. If we observe this development without preconceptions, we can detect a current flowing through the child, from below upward. At first, a young baby, in a state of helplessness, is unable to walk. It has to lie all the time and be carried everywhere. Then, as months pass, we observe a strong force of will, expressed in uncoordinated, jerky movements of the limbs, that gradually leads to the faculty of walking. That powerful force, working upward from the limb system, also works back upon the entire organization of the child.

And, if we make a proper investigation of the metamorphosis of the head, from the stage when the child has to lie all the time and be carried everywhere to the time when it is able to stand on its own legs and walk—which contemporary science also clearly shows us and is obvious physiologically, if we learn to look in the right direction—then we find how what manifests in the child's limb system as the impulse for walking is related to the area of the brain that represents the will organization. We can put this into words as follows. As young children are learning to walk, they are developing in their brains—from below upward, from the lower limbs and in a certain way from the periphery toward the center—their will organization.

In other words: when learning to walk, a child develops the will organization of the brain through the will activity of its lower limbs.

If we now continue our observation of the growing child, we see the next important phase occur in the strengthening of the breathing organization. The breathing assumes what I should like to call a more individual constitution, just as the limb system did through the activity of walking. And this transformation and strengthening of the breathing—which one can observe physiologically—is expressed in the whole activity of *speaking*.

In this instance, there is again a streaming in the human organization from below upward. We can follow quite clearly what a young person integrates into the nervous system by means of language. We can see how, in learning to speak, ever greater inwardness of feeling begins to radiate outward. As a human being, learning to walk becomes integrated into the will sphere of the nervous system, so, in learning to speak, the child's feeling life likewise becomes integrated.

A last stage can be seen in an occurrence that is least observable outwardly and that happens during the second dentition. Certain forces that had been active in the child's organism, indwelling it, come to completion, for the child will not have another change of teeth. The coming of the second teeth reveals that forces that have been at work in the entire organism have come to the end of their task. And so, just as we see that a child's will life is inwardly established through the ability to walk, and that a child's feeling life is inwardly established by its learning to speak so, at the time of the change of teeth, around the seventh year, we see the faculty of mental picturing or *thinking* develop in a more or less individualized form that is no longer bound to the entire bodily organization, as previously.

These are interesting interrelationships that need to be studied more closely. They show how what I earlier called the etheric body works back into the physical body. What happens is that, with the change of teeth, a child integrates the rest of its organization into the head and the nerves.

We can talk about these things theoretically, but nothing is gained by that. Lately, we have become too accustomed to a kind of intellectualism, to certain forces of abstraction, when talking about scientific matters. What I described just now helps you to look at the growing human being not just intellectually: I have been trying to guide you to a more artistic way of observing growing human beings. This involves experiencing how every movement of a child's limbs is integrated into its will organization and how feeling is integrated as the child learns to speak. It is wonderful to see, for example, what happens when someone—perhaps the mother or another—is with the child when it learns to speak the *vowels*. A quality corresponding to the soul being of the adult who is in the child's presence flows into the child's feeling through these vowels. On the other hand, everything that stimulates the child to perform its own movements in relation to the external world—such as finding the right relationship to warmth or coldness—leads to the speaking of *consonants*. It is wonderful to see how one part of the human organism, say moving of limbs or language, works back into another part. As teachers, we meet a child of school age when his or her second teeth are gradually appearing. Just at this time we can see how a force (not unlike latent heat) is liberated from the general growth process of the organism: what previously was at work within the organism is now active in the child's soul life. When we experience all of this, we cannot but feel inspired by what is happening before our eyes.

But these things must not be grasped with the intellect; they must be absorbed with one's whole being. If we do this, then a concrete, artistic sense will pervade our observations of the growing child. Anthroposophy offers practical guidance in recognizing the spirit as it manifests in outer, material processes. Anthroposophy does not want to lead people into any kind of mystical "cloud cuckoo land." It wants to follow the spirit working in matter. In order to be able to do this—to follow the spirit in its creativity, its effectiveness—anthroposophy must stand on firm ground and requires the involvement of whole human beings. In bringing anthroposophy into the field of education, we do not wish to be dogmatic. The Waldorf school is not meant to be an ideological school. It is meant to be a school where what we can gain through anthroposophy with living inwardness can flow into practical teaching methods and actual teaching skills.

What anthroposophy gives as a conception of the world and an understanding of life assigns a special role to the teachers and educators in our school.

Here and there, a certain faith in life beyond death has remained alive in our present culture and civilization. On the other hand, knowledge of human life beyond death up to a new birth on earth has become completely lost.

Anthroposophical research makes it clear that we must speak of human pre-existence, of a soul-spiritual existence before birth. It shows how this can rightly illumine embryology. Today, one considers embryology as if what a human being brought with him into earthly life were merely a matter of heredity, of the physical effects of forces stemming from the child's ancestors. This is quite understandable and we do not wish to remonstrate against such an attitude. In accordance with accepted modern methods, research is done into how the human germ develops in the maternal body. Researchers try to trace in the bodies of the mother and the father, in the parents' bodies, the forces that manifest in the child and so on. But things are just not like that. What is actually happening in the parents' bodies is not a process of construction but, to begin with, one of destruction. Initially, there is a return of the material processes to a state of chaos. And what plays into the body of an expectant mother is the entire cosmos itself.

If one has the necessary basis of observation, one can perceive how the embryo, especially during the first months of pregnancy, is formed not only by the forces of heredity, but by the entire cosmos. The maternal body is in truth the matrix for what is formed through cosmic forces, out of a state of chaos, into the human embryo.

It is quite possible to study these things on the basis of the existing knowledge in physiology, but we will in time regard them from an entirely different viewpoint. We would consider it sheer folly if a physicist claimed, "Here is a magnetic needle, one end of which points north while the opposite end points south: we must look for the force activating the needle within the space of the compass needle itself." That would be considered nonsense in physics. To explain the phenomenon, we must consider the whole earth. We say that the whole earth acts as a kind of magnet, attracting one end of the needle from its north pole and the other from its south pole. In the direction seeking of the compass needle, we observe only one part of a whole complex phenomenon; to understand the whole phenomenon, we must go far beyond the physical boundary of the needle itself. The exact sciences have not yet shown a similar attitude in their investigations of human beings. When studying a most important process, such as the formation of the embryo, the attitude is as limited as if one were to seek the motivating force of a compass needle within the needle itself. That would be considered folly in physics. When we try to discover the forces forming the embryo within the physical boundaries of human beings, we behave just as if we were trying to find the forces moving a compass needle within the physical needle itself. To find the forces forming the human embryo, we must look into the entire cosmos. What works in this way into the embryo is directly linked to the soul-spiritual being of the one to be born as it descends from the soul-spiritual worlds into physical existence.

Here, anthroposophy shows us—however paradoxical it might sound—that, at first, the soul-spiritual part of the human being has *least connection* with the organization of the head. As a baby begins its earthly existence, its prenatal spirit and soul are linked to the rest of the organism excluding the head. The head is a kind of picture of the cosmos but, at the same time, it is the most material part of the body. One could say that at the beginning of human life, the head is least the carrier of the prenatal soul-spiritual life that has come down to begin life on earth.

Those who observe what takes place in a growing child from an anthroposophical point of view see that soul-spiritual qualities, at first concealed in the child, come to the surface in every facial expression, in the entire physiognomy, and in the expression of the child's eyes. They also see how those soul-spiritual elements manifest initially in the development of the limb movements—from crawling to the child's free walking—and next in the impulse to speak, which is closely connected with the respiratory system. They then see how these elements work in the child's organism to bring forth the second teeth. They see, too, how the forces of spirit and soul work upward from below, importing from the outer world what must be taken in unconsciously at first, in order to integrate it then into the most material part of the human being—the organization of the head in thinking, feeling, and willing.

To observe the growing human being in this way, with a scientific artistic eye, indicates the kind of relationship to children that is required if we, their teachers, are to fulfill our tasks adequately as full human beings. A very special inner feeling is engendered when teachers believe that their task is to assist in charming from the child what divine and spiritual beings have sent down from the spiritual world. This task is indeed something that can be brought to new life through anthroposophy.

In our languages, we have a word, an important word, closely allied to the hopes and longings of many people. The word is "immortality." But we will see human life in the right way only after we have a word as fitting for life's beginning as we have for its ending—a word that can become as generally accepted and as commonly used as the word "immortality" (undyingness)—perhaps something like "unbornness." Only if we have such a word will we be able to grasp the full, eternal nature of the human being. Only then will we experience a holy awe and reverence for what lives in the child through the ever creating and working spirit, streaming from below upward. During the first seven years, from birth to the second dentition, the child's soul, together with the spiritual counterpart received from the life before birth, shapes and develops the physical body. At this time, too, the child is most directly linked to its environment.

There is only one word that adequately conveys the mutual relationship of the child to its surroundings at this delicate time of life when thinking, feeling and willing become integrated into the organs—and that word is: *imitation*. During the first period of life, a human being is an imitator *par excellence*. With regard to a child's upbringing, this calls forth one all-important principle: *when you are around a child, only behave in ways that that child can safely imitate*. The impulse to imitate depends on the child's close relationship to its surroundings in which imponderables of soul and spirit play their part.

One cannot communicate with children during these first seven years with admonitions or reprimands. A child of that age cannot learn simply on the authority of a grownup. It learns through imitation. Only if we understand that can we understand a child properly.

Strange things happen—of which I shall give an example that I have given before—when one does not understand this. One day, a father comes saying, "I am so unhappy. My boy, who was always such a good boy, has committed a theft." How should such a case be considered? One asks the worried parent, "How old is your boy and what has he stolen?" The answer comes, "Oh, he is five years old. Until now, he has been such a good child, but yesterday he stole money from his mother. He took it out of the cupboard and bought sweets with it. He did not even eat them himself, but shared them with other boys and girls in the street."

In a case like this, one's response should probably go as follows. "Your boy has not stolen. Most likely, what happened was that he saw his mother every morning taking money from her cupboard to do the shopping for the household. The child's nature is to imitate others, and so the boy did what he had seen his mother do. The concept of stealing is not appropriate in this case. What is appropriate is that—whenever we are in the presence of our children—we do only what they can safely imitate (whether in deeds, gestures, language, or even thought)."

If one knows how to observe such things, one knows that a child imitates in the most subtle, intimate ways. Anyone who acts pedagogically in the manner I have indicated discovers that whatever a child of that age does is based on imitation—even facial expressions. Such imitation continues until a child sheds its milk teeth. Until then, a child's relationship to the surrounding world is extremely direct and real. Children of this age are not yet capable of perceiving with their senses and then judging their perceptions. All of this still remains an undifferentiated process. The child perceives with its senses and, simultaneously, this perception becomes a judgment; and the judgment simultaneously passes into a feeling and a will impulse. They are all one and the same process.

In other words, the child is entirely immersed in the currents of life and has not yet extracted itself from them.

The shedding of the milk teeth marks the first occurrence of this. The forces that had been active in the lower regions of the organism and—following the appearance of the second teeth—are no longer needed there, then manifest as forces in the child's soul-spiritual sphere. At this point, the child enters the second period of life, which begins with the second dentition and ends in puberty. During this second period, the soul and spiritual life of the child becomes liberated, as—under given outer conditions previously cited—latent warmth is liberated. Before this period, we must look in the inner organism, in the organic forming of the physical organism, for the child's soul and spirit.

This is the right way to explore the relationship between body and soul. Principles and relationships of all kinds are being expounded today in theory. According to one, the soul affects the body; according to another, everything that happens in the soul is only an effect of the body. The most frequently held opinion is so-called "psychophysical parallelism," meaning that both types of process—soul-spiritual as well as physical-bodily ones—may be observed side by side. We can speculate at length about the relationship of spirit to body and body to spirit but, if we only speculate and do not engage in careful observation, we will not get beyond mere abstractions. We must not limit our observations to present conditions alone. We must say to ourselves, the forces that we witness as the child's soul spiritual element during the period from the seventh to about the fourteenth year are the same ones that worked before in the lower organism in a hidden or latent way. We must seek in the child's soul and spirit what is at work in the child from birth to the change of teeth and between the change of teeth and puberty. If we do this, we will gain a realistic idea of the relationship between soul and spirit on one side and the physical-bodily processes on the other.

Observe physical processes up to the second dentition and you will find the effects of soul and spirit. But, if you wish to observe the soul and spirit in its own right, then observe a child from the change of teeth until the coming of puberty. Do not proceed by saying, "Here is the body and the soul is somewhere within it; now I wish to find its effects." No, we must now leave the spatial element altogether and enter the dimension of *time.* If we do so, we shall find a true, realistic relationship between body and soul, a relationship that leads to fruitful ideas for life. We shall learn, from a deeper point of view, how to care for a child's physical health *before* the change of teeth, so that the child's psychic and spiritual health can manifest appropriately *afterward,* during the second life period, from the change of teeth to puberty. Similarly, the health of the stomach reveals itself—in the time organism; that is, the etheric or body of formative forces—in the healthy condition of the head. That is the point.

And, if we want to study how to deal with the forces that are released from the physical organism between the change of teeth and puberty—and we are here dealing with one of the most important periods of a child's life, let us call it the time of school duties—I must say, first of all, that they are *formative* forces, liberated formative forces, that have been building up the human organism, *plastically and musically*. We must treat them accordingly. Hence, initially, we must not treat them intellectually. To treat the formerly formative forces, which are now soul-spiritual forces, *artistically*, not intellectually, is the basic demand of anthroposophical pedagogy.

The essence of Waldorf education is to make education into an art—the art of the right treatment of children, if I may use the expression. A teacher must be an artist, for it is the teacher's task to deal in the right way with the forces that previously shaped the child's organism. Such forces need to be treated artistically—no matter which subject the teacher is to introduce to children entering the Waldorf school. Practically, this means that we begin not with reading but with writing—but learning to write must in no way be an intellectual pursuit. We begin by letting our young pupils draw and paint patterns and forms that are attuned to their will lives. Indeed, watching these lessons, many people would feel them to be rather a strange approach to this fundamental subject!

Each teacher is given complete freedom. We do not insist on a fixed pedagogical dogma but, instead, we introduce our teachers to the whole spirit of anthroposophical pedagogical principles and methods. For instance, if you were to enter a first grade class, you might see how one teacher has his or her pupils move their arms in the air to given rhythms. Eventually each pupil will then draw these on paper in the simplest form. Hence, out of the configuration of the physical organism—that is, out of the sphere of the children's will—we elicit something that quite naturally assumes an artistic form and we gradually transform such patterns into the forms of letters. In this way, learning to write avoids all abstraction. Rather, writing arises in the same way as it originally entered human evolution. First, there was picture-writing, which was a direct result of outer reality. Then, gradually, this changed into our written symbols, which have become completely abstract. Thus, beginning with a pictorial element, we lead into the modern alphabet, which speaks to the intellect. Only after having first taught writing out of such artistic activities do we introduce reading. If teachers approach writing and reading in this way, working from an artistic realm and meeting the child with artistic intentions, they are able to appeal above all to a child's forces of will. It is out of the will forces that, fundamentally speaking, all psychological and intellectual development must unfold. But, moving from writing to reading, a teacher is aware of moving from what is primarily a willing activity to one that has more of a feeling quality. The children's thinking, for its part, can be trained by dealing with numbers in arithmetic.

If teachers are able to follow a child's whole soul-spiritual configuration in detail as each child first draws single figures, which leads to formation of letters and then to writing words that are also read—and if they are able to pursue this whole process with anthroposophical insight and observation of growing human beings—then a true practice of teaching will emerge.

Only now can we see the importance of applying an artistic approach during the first years of school. Everything that is brought to a child through music in a sensible and appropriate way will show itself later as initiative. If we restrict a child's assimilation of the musical element appropriate to the seventh to eighth year, we are laming the development of that child's initiative, especially in later life. A true teacher of our time must never lose sight of the whole complex of such interconnections. There are many other things—we shall have to say more about them later—that must be observed not only year by year but week by week during the life period from the change of teeth to puberty.

There is one moment of special importance, approximately halfway through the second life period; that is, roughly between the ninth and tenth years. This is a point in a child's development that teachers need to observe particularly carefully. If one has attained real insight into human development and is able to observe the time organism or etheric body, as I have described it, throughout the course of human life, one knows how, in old age, when a person is inclined to look back over his or her life down to early childhood days, among the many memory pictures that emerge, there emerge particularly vividly the pictures of teachers and other influential figures of the ninth and tenth years.

These more intimate details of life tend to be overlooked by natural-scientific methods of research that concentrate on more external phenomena. Unfortunately, not much attention is paid to what happens to a child—earlier in one child, later in another—approximately between the ninth and tenth years. What enters a child's unconscious then emerges again vividly in old age, creating either happiness or pain, and generating either an enlivening or a deadening effect. This is an exact observation. It is neither fantasy nor mere theory. It is a realization that is of immense importance for the teacher. At this age, a child has specific needs that, if heeded, help bring about a definite relationship between the pupil and the teacher.

A teacher simply has to observe the child at this age to sense how a more or less innate and unspoken question lives in the child's soul at this time, a question that can never be put into actual words. And so, if the child cannot ask the question directly, it is up to the teacher to bring about suitable conditions for a constructive resolution of this situation.

What is actually happening here?

One would hardly expect a person who, in the 1890's [1894], wrote a book entitled *The Philosophy of Freedom*[4] to advocate the principle of authority on any conservative or reactionary grounds. Yet, from the standpoint of child development alone, it must be said that, just as up to the change of teeth a child is a being who *imitates*, so, after this event, a child needs naturally to look up to the *authority* of the teacher and educator. This requires of the teacher the ability to command natural respect, so that a pupil accepts truths coming from the teacher simply because of the child's loving respect, not on the strength of the child's own judgments. A great deal depends on that.

Again, this is a case in which we need to have had personal experience. We must know from experience what it means for a child's whole life—and for the constitution of a person's soul—when children hear people talk of a highly respected member of their family, whom they have not yet met, but about whom all members of the household speak in hushed reverential tones as a wise, good, or for any other reason highly esteemed family member. The moment then arrives when the child is to be introduced to such a person for the first time. The child feels overcome by deep awe. He or she hardly dares open the door to enter into the presence of such a personality. Such a child feels too shy to touch the person's hand. If we have lived through such an experience, if our souls have been deepened in childhood in this way, then we know that this event created a lasting impression and entered the very depths of our consciousness, to resurface at a later age. This kind of experience must become

4. Published (1995) as *Intuitive Thinking as a Spiritual Path.*

the keynote of the relationship between the teacher and the child. Between the change of teeth and puberty, a child should willingly accept whatever the teacher says on the strength of such a natural sense of authority.

An understanding of this direct elemental relationship can help a teacher become a real artist in the sense that I have already indicated.

During this same period, however, another feeling also lives in the child, often only dimly and vaguely felt. This is the feeling that those who are the objects of such authority must themselves also look up to something higher. A natural outcome of this direct, tangible relationship between the teacher and the child is the child's awareness of the teacher's own religious feelings and of the way in which the teacher relates to the metaphysical world-all. Such imponderables must not be overlooked in teaching and education. People of materialistic outlook usually believe that whatever affects children reaches them only through words or outer actions. Little do they know that quite other forces are at work in children!

Let us consider something which occasionally happens. Let us assume that a teacher thinks "I—as teacher—am an intelligent person, but my pupils are very ignorant. If I want to communicate a feeling for the immortality of the human soul to my students, I can think, for instance, of what happens when a butterfly emerges from a chrysalis. I can compare this event, this picture, with what happens when a person dies. Thus I can say to my children, 'Just as the butterfly flies out of the chrysalis, so, after death, the immortal soul leaves the physical body.' Such a comparison, I am certain, offers a useful simile for the child's benefit."

But if the picture—the simile—is chosen with an attitude of mental superiority on the part of the teacher, we find that it does not touch the pupils at all and, soon after hearing it, they forget all about it, *because the teacher did not believe in the truth of his simile.*

Anthroposophy teaches us to believe in such a picture and I can assure you that, for me, the butterfly emerging from the chrysalis is not a simile that I have invented. For me, the butterfly emerging out of the chrysalis is a revelation on a lower plane of what on a higher level represents the immortality of the human soul. As far as I am concerned, it is not I who created this picture out of my own reasoning; rather, it is the world itself that reveals the processes of nature in the emergence of a butterfly. That is what this picture means to me. I believe with every fibre of my soul that it represents a truth placed by the gods themselves before our eyes. I do not imagine that, compared with the child, I am wiser and the chid more foolish. I believe in the truth of this picture with the same earnestness that I wish to awaken in the child. If a teacher teaches with such an attitude, the child will remember it for the rest of his or her life.

Unseen supersensible—or shall we say imponderable—forces are at work here. It is not the words that we speak to children that matter, but what we ourselves are—and above all what we are when we are dealing with our children. This is especially important during the period between the ninth and tenth years, for it is during this time that the child feels the underlying background out of which a teacher's words are spoken. Goethe said: "Consider well the *what,* but consider more the *how.*"[5] A child can see whether an adult's words express a genuine relationship with the supersensible world or whether they are spoken with a materialistic attitude—the words have a different "ring." The child experiences a difference of quality between the two approaches. During this period between the ninth and tenth years, children need to feel, if only subconsciously, that as

5. "Das Was bedenke, mehr bedenke Wie"—*Faust II,* Laboratory Scene.

they look up to the authority of their teachers, their teacher likewise looks up to what no longer is outwardly visible. Then, through the relationship of teacher to child, a feeling for other people becomes transformed into a religious experience.

This, in turn, is linked to other matters—for example, the child's ability to differentiate itself from its surroundings. This too is an inner change, requiring a change of approach toward the subjects taught. We shall speak of that tomorrow. In the meantime, one can see how important it is that certain moods of soul—certain soul conditions—form an intimate part of the theory and the practice of education.

When the plans for founding the Waldorf school in Stuttgart were nearing realization, the question of how to form the hearts and the souls of teachers so that they entered their classrooms and greeted their children in the right spirit was considered most important. I value my task of having to guide this school enormously. I also value the fact that, when I have been able to be there in person, the attitude about which I have been speaking has been much in evidence among the teaching staff, however varied the individual form of expression. Having heard what I have had to tell you, you now will realize the significance of a question that I always ask, not in the same words but in different ways each time, either during festive school occasions or when visiting different classes. The question is, "Children, do you love your teachers?" And the children respond "Yes!" in chorus with a sincere enthusiasm that reveals the truth of their answer. Breathing through all of those children's souls, one can feel the existence of a bond of deep inner affection between teachers and pupils and that the children's feeling for the authority of the teacher has become a matter of course. Such natural authority is meant to form the essence of our educational practice during these years of childhood.

Waldorf pedagogy is thus built not only upon principles and educational axioms—of which, thanks to the work of the great pedagogues, there are plenty in existence already—but, above all, upon the pedagogical skills in practical classroom situations, that is, the way each individual teacher handles his or her class. Such skill is made possible by what anthroposophy unfolds in the human soul and in the human heart. What we strive for is a pedagogy that is truly an art, an art arising from educational methods and principles founded on anthroposophy.

Of course, with such aims today, one must be prepared to make certain compromises. Hence, when the Waldorf school was opened, I had to come to the following arrangement with the school authorities. In a memorandum, worked out when the school was founded, I stipulated that our pupils should attain standards of learning comparable to those reached in other schools by the age of nine, so that, if they wanted, they would be able to transfer into the same class in another school. But, during the intervening years—that is, from when they entered school around six to the age of nine—I asserted our complete freedom to use teaching time according to our own methods and pedagogical point of view. The same arrangement was offered to pupils who stayed in the school through the age of twelve. Because they had reached the standards of learning generally expected at that age, they were again given the possibility of entering the appropriate classes in other schools.

The same thing happens again when our pupils reach puberty; that is, when they reach school-leaving age.[6] But what happens in between is left entirely to our discretion. Hence we are able to ensure that it unfolds out of our anthroposophical understanding of human beings, just as our curriculum and educational aims do, which are likewise created entirely out of

6. In 1921, the school-leaving age in Germany was fourteen.

the child's nature. And we try of course to realize these aims while leaving scope for individual differences. Even in comparatively large classes, the individuality of each single pupil is still allowed to play its proper part.

Tomorrow, we shall see what an incisive point of time the twelfth year is.

There is obviously a certain kind of perfection in education that will be attained only when we are no longer restricted by such compromises—when we are given complete freedom to deal with pupils all of the way from the change of teeth to puberty. Tomorrow, I shall indicate how this could be done. All the same, since life itself offered us the opportunity to do so, an attempt had to be made. Anthroposophy never seeks to demonstrate a theory—this always tends toward intellectuality—but seeks to engage directly in the fullness of practical life. It seeks to reveal something that will expand the scope of human beings and call into play the full potential of each individual. Certainly, in general terms, such demands have been made before. The *what* is known; with the help of anthroposophy, we must find the *how*. Today, I was able to give you a few indications regarding children up to the ninth year or so. When we meet again tomorrow, I shall speak in greater detail about the education of our children during the succeeding years.

6

Educational Methods Based on Anthroposophy

CHRISTIANIA (OSLO) — NOVEMBER 24, 1921

PART II

Yesterday, I sought to show how the philosophy and practice of an education based on anthroposophy rest on an intimate knowledge of human beings and hence also of growing human beings or children. I tried to show how a growing child can be regarded as a sort of "time-organism," so that we must always bear in mind that the activities of each succeeding year of a child's development occur against the background of that child's entire life. We can therefore plant something like soul-spiritual seeds in our children that will bear fruits of inner happiness and security in practical life situations for the rest of their earthly existences.

First, we looked at the period between birth and the change of teeth, when a child is a completely imitative being. We must realize that, during this first period of life, a young child is connected to its environment in an extremely intimate way. In a manner of speaking, everything that happens through the people around the young child, even their thoughts and feelings, affects the child in such a way that it grows into the happenings in its surrounding world by imitating them. This relationship—this connection to the surrounding world—has a kind of polar opposite in what happens during puberty.

Naturally, during the present age, with its materialistic overtones, there is much talk of the process of puberty. The phenomenon is usually viewed as an isolated event; however, to unprejudiced observation, it must be seen rather as a consequence of a complete metamorphosis of the whole course of life thus far. At this age, human beings develop not only their more or less soul-spiritual or physically colored erotic feelings but also their personal relationship to the external world. This begins with the forming of judgments that express themselves in strong sympathies and antipathies. Basically, it is only now that young people are placed fully within the world. Only at puberty do they attain the maturity to turn toward the world in such a way that independent thinking, feeling, and judgment can live within them.

During the years between the change of teeth and puberty, a child's relationship to its teacher is based above all on the feeling of respect for the teacher's authority. Those important years can be regarded as lying between two polar opposites. One of them is the age of childhood when, without any subjective awareness, a child lives wholly within its outer surroundings. The other is the time of sexual maturity or puberty. At this time, adolescents as subjects differentiate themselves from the world—with all their newly awakened inwardness—by what could be called in the broadest sense sympathies and antipathies. In short, they distinguish themselves from the world by what we might call the various manifestations, or revelations, of love.

Between these two poles lies the lower school and, as teachers, it is our task to create a bridge from one pole to the other by means of education. During both stages—during early childhood as well as during puberty—the growing person finds a certain foothold in life, in childhood through union with the surrounding world and later through the feeling of being anchored within the self. The intervening years, encompassing the actual lower-school years, are the time when the growing child is in an unstable equilibrium, needing the support of the teacher and educator. Basically, during those years of primary education, the teacher stands as a representative of the entire world in the eyes of the child. That world is not one of mere arbitrary coincidence but rather the natural, lawful order in human development that is brought to life in what the teacher and educator means to the child. For the child, the teacher represents the whole world. Happy are those children who—before they must find a personal relation to the world by means of individual judgments, will impulses, and feelings—receive the world through someone in whom the world is rightly reflected!

This is a deeply felt premise of the education that is to be based on anthroposophy. With this principle, we try to gain insight into the child's development, month by month, even week by week, in such intimate ways that we become able to read the curriculum and all our educational aims directly from the nature of the growing child. I could summarize this by saying: knowledge of the human being that is true and intimate also means knowledge of how and when—during which year and even during which month—to introduce the appropriate subject matter.

We must consider that until about the age of seven—and children should not really enter school before that age—a child lives entirely by imitation. Our young pupils are beings who strive with their will to be at one with their surroundings. This fact alone should preclude any appeal to the intellect, which depends on the soul's self activity. Nor should we appeal to the child's personal feelings, which in any case are in complete sympathy with the environment. If we bear in mind that every response of such an imitative being bears a will character, we will realize how strongly the innate will nature meets us when we receive a child into school at the time of the second dentition.

Above all, then, we must begin by educating, instructing—training—the child's will. This in itself implies an emphasis on an artistic approach. For instance, when teaching writing, we do not immediately introduce the letters of the alphabet in their present form, because these have already become quite alienated from human nature. Rather, we begin by letting the children paint and draw, an activity that is a natural consequence and externalization of their will activities and that in turn leads to writing.

Proceeding in this way, a teacher notices in the children two different tendencies that should be given consideration. For whether we contribute to a child's future health or lack of health depends upon how we deal with these two tendencies. In relation to writing, we find two types of child. This becomes especially evident when we guide them toward writing through a kind of painting. One type of child learns to write in a way that always retains a quality of painting. This child writes "with the eye," observing every line and working with an aesthetic feeling for the beauty of the form—a painterly quality lives in all his or her writing. The other type forms the letters on the paper more mechanically, with a certain compulsion. Even in writing lessons—often given for dubious pedagogical reasons, especially in the case of older persons who believe that they must improve their handwriting—the aim is usually to enable the participants to put their letters on paper with this mechanical kind of compulsion. This is how individual handwriting is developed. Just as people have their gestures, of which they are unaware, so too they have their handwriting, of which they are equally unaware. Those who write mechanically no longer experience an echo of their writing. Their gaze does not rest upon it with an aesthetic pleasure. They do not bring an artistic element of drawing into their writing.

Each child ought to be guided toward introducing this artistic element into handwriting. A child's eye should always rest on the piece of paper on which he or she is writing and so receive an impression of all that is being put into the writing. This will avoid writing under sheer inner mechanical compulsion, but will allow the child to experience an echo of his or her writing and the various letters. If we do this, we shall be cultivating a certain love in the child for what surrounds it—a sense of responsibility for its surroundings. Although this remark might sound improbable, it is nevertheless true. A caring attitude for whatever we do in life is a direct consequence of this way of learning to write—a method in which writing is a matter not only of manual dexterity but also for the eyes, for aesthetic seeing and willing.

We should not underestimate how such familiar things influence the whole of human life. Many persons who, later in life, appear lacking in a sense of responsibility—lacking in loving devotion to the surrounding world—would have been helped if they had been taught writing in the right way.

We must not overlook such intimate interconnections in education. Anthroposophy therefore seeks to shed light on all aspects of human nature—not just theoretically but *lovingly.* It tries to recognize the inherent soul and spiritual background of all external human traits and this allows it to add a completely practical dimension to the education of the young. If we remember to allow a child's forces of will to flow into such activities as writing, then learning to write—writing lessons—will eventually produce fruits of the kind I previously mentioned.

After writing, we proceed to reading lessons. Reading involves a child's life of feeling to a greater extent than writing and ought to develop from writing. Reading entails a greater element of observation, while writing is more a matter of active participation. But the starting point in education should always be an appeal to the will element, to active participation, and not only to powers of observation.

Three steps should always be followed when teaching children aged from seven to fourteen. First, the aim should be to involve the will; that is, the active participation of the pupils. Second, the aim is gradually to lead toward what becomes an attitude of observation. And only during the last phase of this period do we proceed to the third step, that of making of experiments, to experimentation.

Yesterday, I drew your attention to an important moment occurring between the ninth and tenth years. I pointed to the fact that much depends on a teacher's detecting the inner soul needs of each child at this critical stage and taking appropriate action. This moment in a child's development must be observed accurately. For only at this stage does the child begin to learn to differentiate its individual self from its surroundings. It does this in three ways—in feeling, in will activity, and through the forming of judgments. The ability to distinguish between self and environment with full inner independence is achieved only at puberty.

Between the ninth and tenth years, a first harbinger of this separation from the surrounding world already begins to make itself felt. It is so important—just because we must support a child's being until puberty—that we recognize this moment and adapt our teaching accordingly. Up to this age, it is best not to expect children to distinguish themselves from their surroundings. We are always at a disadvantage when we as teachers introduce subjects—such as the study of nature—that require a certain objectivity, an inner distancing of the self from its surroundings, before a child is nine or ten. The more teachers imbue the surrounding world with human qualities, the more they speak about it pictorially, and the more they employ an artistic approach, the better it is for the inner unfolding of their pupils' will natures. For, by becoming directly involved, these will natures are also thereby inwardly strengthened.

Everything musical helps deepen a child's will nature. After age six or seven, the element of music helps make a child more inward, more soulful. The will itself is strengthened by all pictorial and artistic activities—but only, of course, as long as they correspond to the child's age. Naturally, we cannot yet speak about plants, animals, or even lifeless objects, as something independent and separate. On the contrary, a child should feel that such things are an extension of its own being. Personification of outer objects and facts is right and appropriate during this time of a child's life.

We are wrong to believe that, when we personify nature, we are presenting a child with something untrue. Arguments of this kind have no validity. Our attitude should be, "What must I bring to a child to liberate his or her life forces? What can I do so that what is within rises to the surface of life?" We can help this happen, above all, by being as lively as possible in our descriptions and stories of the surrounding world—if we make the whole surrounding world appear as if it issues from a human being's inner self. Everything introduced to the child at this age should be addressed to the child's whole being, not just to its head and nervous systems.

A false conception of human nature and an entirely misguided picture of human beings underlie current attitudes toward education. We have a false anthropology that overemphasizes the nervous system. Rather, it is of prime importance that we recognize a current flowing through the entire person from below upward—from the activity of the limbs and from everything that follows from our relationship to the external world—that impresses itself into the nervous system and particularly into the brain. From this perspective, anthroposophical anthropology is not being paradoxical when it maintains that, if a child practices the appropriate movements at an earlier age, he or she will develop intelligence, intellect, the power of reasoning, the ability to discriminate, and so forth at a later age. If we are asked, "Why has a particular child not developed a healthy ability to discriminate by the time he or she is thirteen or fourteen? Why does he or she make such confused judgments?" We often have to answer, "Because the child was not encouraged to make the right kinds of physical hand and foot movement in early childhood."

The fact that eurythmy is a required subject in the Waldorf curriculum shows that, from our point of view, these remarks are justified. Eurythmy is an art of movement but it is also of great pedagogical value. Eurythmy is truly a visible language. It is not like mime, nor is it a form of dance. Rather, eurythmy originates in the perception of tendencies toward movement in the human being that may be observed—if I may borrow Goethe's expression—with "sensible-supersensible beholding." Those tendencies toward movement (I say "tendencies" rather than the actual movements themselves) are seen when human beings express themselves in speech, with the larynx and other speech organs performing the actual movements.

Those movements are transformed into moving air, which in turn becomes the carrier of sound and tone perceived by the ear. But there exist other inner tendencies or inclinations toward movement which proceed no further than the nascent state and yet can be studied by "sensible-supersensible beholding." It is possible to study what is formed in a human being but never becomes an actual movement, being instead transformed, or metamorphosed, into movement of the larynx and the other speech organs.

In eurythmy, the movements are performed by one person or by groups whose movements produce an ordered, organic, and visible form of speech, just as human speech organs produce audible speech or song. Each single movement—every detail of movement that is performed eurythmically— manifests such laws of the human organism as are found in speech or song.

This is why, in the Waldorf school, we witness again and again how—provided that it is taught properly—younger children in the first eight grades find their way into eurythmy, this new language, quite naturally. Just as, at this stage of development, a child's organism desires to move through imitation, so likewise is the child naturally inclined to reveal itself through the language of eurythmy. A sense of inner well being depends on the possibility of the child's expressing itself through this medium. Older pupils develop the same inner response toward this visible language of eurythmy, only in a metamorphosed form, at a later stage. Indeed, we find that, just as eurythmy has been called forth from the inner order governing the human organism, it works back upon the human organization in a healthy manner.

For the moment, let us consider the human form. Let us take as an example the outer human form—although it would be equally possible to take the forms of inner organs—but let us for the moment take the human hand together with its arm. Can we really understand the form of the human hand and arm when they are in a position of rest? It would be an illusion to think that we could. We can understand the forms of the fingers, of the palm, and of the arm only when we see them in movement. The resting form only makes sense when it begins to move. We could say that the hand at rest owes its form to the hand in movement and that the movements of the hand or arm must be as they are because of the form of the resting hand.

In the same way, one can summon forth from the whole human being the movements, like those connected with the vowels and consonants, that originate in the inner organization and are determined by the natural organization or form of the human being. Eurythmy has been created in harmony with the innate laws of the human form. A child experiences the change of the human form at rest into the form in movement—the meaningful transition into visible speech through eurythmy—with deep inner satisfaction and is thereby enabled to experience the inner life of its whole being. And this works back again in that the entire organism activates what is later transformed into intelligence in a way that should not be activated by anything else. If we try to develop a child's intelligence *directly*, we always introduce a more or less deadening or laming agent into its development. But, if we cultivate intelligence through the whole human being, then we proceed in a fundamentally healing manner. We endow the child with a form of intelligence that grows easily from the whole human being, whereas onesided training of the intellect resembles something artificially grafted onto the organism.

When seen in its practical pedagogical context, eurythmy—which is an obligatory subject along with lessons in gymnastics—therefore has the effect of ensouled gymnastics. I feel sure that the time will come when people will think about such matters more openly and more freely than is usual today.

In this respect, something extraordinary happened to me a short time ago. I talked about ideas concerning eurythmy and there happened to be in the audience someone who could rightly be called one of the most eminent Central European physiologists. You would be surprised if I mentioned his name, for he is a world-famous personality. On this occasion, out of a certain modesty, I said that anthroposophy does not clamor for revolutionary aims in any subject. I said that, one day, one might come to think of gymnastics as having been evoked from human physiology, from the inherent law and order of the physical body, and that, in that sense, it can be said to have a beneficial effect on the healthy development of the human physical body. I continued by saying that this more spiritual, ensouled eurythmy will find its proper place side by side with gymnastics because, in eurythmy, although due consideration is given to the physical aspects, at the same time, in each movement performed, an element of soul and spirit also lives, allowing the child to experience meaningful soul and spiritual sense and never merely empty physical movements. The child always experiences how the inner being of the eurythmist flows into the movements performed. And the strange thing was that this famous physiologist came to see me afterward and said, "You called gymnastics an educational aid. But I entirely disagree with your justification of gymnastics on physiological grounds. From my point of view, I consider gymnastic lessons for children to be pure barbarism!"

Well, I would never have dreamed of making such a statement myself, but I nevertheless find it interesting to hear what one of the most eminent physiologists of our time has to say about this subject. As I mentioned before, I do not wish to go as far as this physiologist but merely wish to say that eurythmy has its own contribution to make in practical pedagogy, side by side with gymnastic lessons as they are given today.

By working back again on the spirit and the soul of children up to the ages of nine and ten, eurythmy becomes an important educational aid. The same applies to later years when, between nine and ten, a child learns to discriminate between the self and the external world. Here, however, one must be very careful about how such discrimination occurs. First, one must be careful not to introduce subject matter that predominantly activates a child's intellect and faculty of cognition.

From this point of view, before proceeding to mineralogy, physics, and chemistry, it is good to introduce first animal and then plant study. Through the study of zoology and botany, children learn to discriminate between the inner and outer worlds in new and different ways. According to a given child's own nature, it might feel more akin to the animal world than to the plant kingdom. Pupils experience the plant world as a revelation of the outer world. On the other hand, with regard to the animal kingdom, children feel greater, more immediate rapport, inwardly sensing that there are similarities in many respects between animals and human beings. Teachers should definitely be aware of this when giving lessons in zoology and botany. Hence, when introducing botany, they should relate the plants to the earth as to a living organism. They should speak of the earth as a living organism. They should speak of it during the different seasons and of how it reveals itself by appropriate plant growth at different times of the year. In other words, they should introduce a temporal aspect into the study of plants.

The use of observational methods, while justifiable in other situations, can easily be disturbing if applied to botany and zoology. Generally speaking, far too little attention is given to the fact that the earth forms a unity with its plant growth. Again, you might find this paradoxical, but just as we can hardly study the organization of an animal's or a human being's hair separately—having rather to consider it in connection with the whole organism, as part of a whole—so we should also consider the earth as an organism, and the plant world as part of it. If we introduce botany in this manner, a child, observing the plant kingdom, will differentiate its own being from the plant world in the right way.

On the other hand, the approach to animal study should be very different. Children feel a natural kinship, a "soul-bridge," with the animal world and this feeling of kinship should be taken into account. The opinions of older nature philosophers are often smiled at today. But you will find all of the opinions of these older nature philosophers in Goethe's way of looking at the animal world. According to the Goethean way, we look at the form of an animal and find, for instance, that in the form of the lion the development of the chest and the heart predominate, whereas, in the case of other animals, the digestive organs may predominate; in still other species, the teeth are especially developed, or the horns, and so on. We consider the various animal forms as expressions of single organs. In other words, we could say that there are head animals, chest animals, and limb animals. Indeed, one could arrange the various animal forms according to even more subdivisions. This gives us the totality. Finally, taking all of the various animal forms together—synthesizing them in such a way that what predominates in a particular species regresses to fit itself back into a whole—we come to the form of a human being. From the point of view of outer form, therefore, the human being represents a synthesis of the entire animal world.

It is quite possible to call forth in the child a feeling for this synthesis of the entire animal kingdom in humanity. If we do this, we have achieved something very significant, for we have then allowed the child to relate both to the plant world and to the animal world in the right way. In the case of the animal world, the child can learn to see a human being spread across the entire animal kingdom and in the plant kingdom something that belongs organically to the whole earth. If, by giving individual examples, we can bring to life such a study of animals or plants at a deeper level, we respect at the same time how human beings should fit rightly into the world according to their inner nature. Then, just at the age when a child learns to differentiate itself from its surrounding world by beginning to discriminate between subject and object, she or he will grow into the world in the right way. Through the study of botany, we can succeed in separating the outer world from the inner life of a human being in the right way, and at the same time enable a child to build bridges into the world. Such bridges are essential if a right feeling for the world, if love for the world, is to develop. We can also do this by presenting the animal world to the child in the form of a picture of the human being unfolded or outspread. Doing this, we are following an organic, living path by allowing the child to find its proper relationship to living nature. Only when the twelfth year begins can we cultivate purely intellectual work and appeal to the powers of reasoning without harming a child's development.

When the curriculum that I have outlined today is followed, we begin by cultivating the life of the will. By presenting the child's relationship to the plant world and to the animal world in nature study, we begin the cultivation of the child's feeling life. The child then learns to relate to the plant and animal kingdoms not just theoretically. Indeed, the concepts gained from these lessons lay the foundations for a deeper relationship to the whole surrounding world. Something happens here that really touches the child's feeling, the child's psyche. And this is of immense importance; for, proceeding thus by engaging the child in the right kind of movement, and guiding and cultivating children's will forces and their lives of heart and soul up to almost the twelfth year, we can then find the transition to the actual cultivation of the intellect by introducing subject matter belonging to lifeless, inorganic nature.

Mineralogy, physics, and chemistry should not be introduced before this age (the twelfth year). The only intellectual occupation not harmful during the earlier ages is arithmetic. This can be practiced earlier because it is directly connected with an inner discipline and because it is neutral with regard to the cultivation of both will and heart or soul. Of course, it depends entirely on our knowing how to activate the child outwardly through the right kind of geometry and arithmetic during the age when the child is at the stage of authority.

Regarding the introduction of subjects belonging to inanimate nature, we should wait until approximately the twelfth year. Thus our ability to read in a child's nature what can and should be taught at each appropriate age is the whole point around which we form our curriculum.

If we introduce children to the external world in this way, we may be certain that we are preparing them for the practical sides of life also. Unfortunately, our present civilization does little to guide people into dealing with practical life. Rather, they are led into a routine life, the practical aspects of which consist in their being able to manipulate a few skills in a more or less mechanical fashion. Real love for practical work, love for working with one's hands, even if only crude and simple skills are required, is poorly cultivated by our present educational methods.

Yet, if we teach from insight into human nature, we will find a way to develop a genuine impulse to become practical people in those pupils who have reached puberty. For this reason, we introduce practical subjects in the Waldorf school as soon as our pupils reach puberty. We try to teach them crafts, which at the same time demand an artistic treatment.

The Waldorf school is a coeducational school and this policy has not thus far shown the slightest disadvantage from a pedagogical point of view. But what has also emerged is that boys love to do so-called "girls'" jobs—such as knitting, crocheting, and so on—and that it is precisely in these practical lessons that boys and girls in the Waldorf school work harmoniously together. You will perhaps forgive me for making a personal remark: men who as boys were taught to knit at school will know how much these skills have contributed to their ability to work with their heads and how their dexterity in using knitting needles, in threading darning needles, and so on has been transmuted into the development of logical thinking. This may sound peculiar to you, but it nevertheless belongs to one of the more hidden facts of life.

The origin of poor or faulty thinking is by no means always to be found in a person's innate intellectual capacities. What, during a person's adult life, is revealed as human intelligence, must be traced back to the whole human being. Above all, we must realize that what is expressed through practical activities is intimately connected not only to the human head itself, but also to the way in which it has an effect on all that belongs generally to the cultivation of the sphere of the head.

If insight into the human being based on anthroposophy is to enter the field of education, it must guide the child towards a practical and realistic conception of life. Anthroposophy does not wish to lead anyone into a mystical "cloud cuckoo land." It does not wish to alienate people from practical life. On the contrary, it seeks to lead human beings into the fullness of practical life so that they really begin to love practical work. For instance, in my opinion, one cannot be a true philosopher unless one is also capable of making a pair of shoes somehow or other, if the situation demands it, and unless one is capable of taking full part in all human activities. All specialization, however necessary it might be in life, can work in a healing way only if people are able to stand fully in life, at least to a certain degree. Naturally, not every adult can do this. Nevertheless, such is our aim in education, as I have taken the liberty of presenting it to you.

If we have thus guided our pupils from "doing" to observing and, finally, to practical participation, which includes the making of scientific experiments—that is, if we have guided our pupils starting from training their will lives through observation permeated by human feeling and finally to more intellectual work—if we have done all this, then we have followed a curriculum capable of planting seeds in their souls and spirits that will bear fruit throughout their lives. It is this wholeness of life that teachers must bear in mind at all times.

A great deal of thought has gone into finding the origin of morality. Ours is a time of abstraction: we philosophize about how human awareness of morality has found its way into life and where it is found in the individual and in the life of society. But so far, because our time is one of intellectualism and abstraction, we have not found its source in realistic terms. Let us seriously consider the idea that it is in the nature of the child, between second dentition and puberty, to surrender freely to the authority of a teacher who represents the whole world to the child. And let us accept that the child receives everything that enters its soul under the influence of this authority. If we do that, then we will adopt this line of thought in our education to give the child a picture of the educator and teacher as a living example of morality, one in which morality is personified. Listen carefully to what I say: teachers do not implant an ethical attitude by moralizing. To the child, they are morality personified, so that there is truly no need for them to moralize. Whatever they do will be considered right; whatever they refrain from doing will be considered wrong. Thus, in living contact between child and teacher, an entire system of sympathies and antipathies regarding matters of life will develop. Through those sympathies and antipathies, a right feeling for the dignity of human beings and for a proper involvement in life will develop. At this age, too, we can perhaps see emerging from the inner depths of the child's soul something that surfaces at times and needs only to be interpreted correctly.

We can observe how, under the influence of certain feelings, a child blushes. The most significant cause for blushing is a sense of shame. I am not thinking here of shame in its more restricted, sex-related sense. I am speaking of shame in a wide and general sense. For example, when a child has done something that, according to the system of sympathies and antipathies that it has developed, must appear wrong or bad, a feeling of shame is provoked. It is as if the child wanted to hide from the world. In such a situation, life-sustaining blood rushes into the periphery. It is as if the real soul of the child were trying to hide itself behind the blushing. The other extreme can be seen when a child must face a danger threatening from outside. We then see a paling in the child's countenance. These two phenomena—blushing and paling in the human face—point to something of great significance; they point to the system of sympathies and antipathies.

My point is that, if we follow up this blushing and paling in a child's soul, we find the consequences of what teachers and educators have cultivated in the field of education during the period between a child's second dentition and puberty. It is a question not of teaching morals, but of living morally. Through the relationship between the teacher and the child, what is good crosses over into the realm of sympathies and antipathies. They express themselves outwardly in paling and blushing, which are generated by the soul either when the inner life of feeling is threatened, destroyed, or paralysed, or when it feels a sense of shame. As a result, the appropriate feeling, or an entire complex of feelings for a genuine and true human dignity, is engendered in the child. It is of paramount importance that a living morality develop in this changeable, mobile relationship between child and teacher. Remember that yesterday I characterized the member of the human organism that works in time as the etheric body. When the child reaches sexual maturity, another, higher member of the human organism comes to meet the etheric body. That is, during the age of sexual maturity, the human astral body, as it is called in anthroposophy, comes to meet the etheric body. This is a stage when what had developed into a system of sympathies and antipathies in the child changes into a person's moral attitudes. It is the astral body that places human beings within the world. It holds and gathers the person together far more tightly than the etheric body. What was previously a system of sympathies and antipathies, cultivated by the teacher's artistic approach, now becomes transmuted into a moral attitude of soul.

This is the wonderful secret of puberty. It is the metamorphosis of what had previously lived in the child as living morality into a conscious sense of morality and of moral principles. That metamorphosis takes place on a comprehensive scale. The erotic side plays merely a subordinate role. Only a materialistic age sees the most important issue in a sexual context. The true and fundamental aspect of the change must be seen in the wonderful secret that what is at first founded in a natural way through a child's direct and immediate experience now sees the light of day in a conscious sense of morality.

Just as a plant is rooted in the ground, so everything pertaining to a conscious sense of morality in the world—everything of an ethical nature living in society and social life generally—is rooted just as firmly as the plant is rooted in the ground in what was cultivated artistically and aesthetically into a system of sympathies and antipathies between the second dentition and puberty.

Instead of trying to find the origin of human goodness in philosophical abstractions, it is more productive to observe concrete realities. We can answer the question, "What is goodness in real life?" by saying that goodness in real life is the outcome of what we adults were able to nourish by means of our pupils' sense of authority during the period that we are discussing.

In this way, we observe life as a whole. We observe the situation of the child during the school years of inner consolidation. During those years, the child's soul is still intimately connected with the physical organism. Only at the age of about 35, does a person's soul begin to loosen itself somewhat from the physical body. At that point, two ways are open to us—although, unfortunately, all too often there remains no choice. At that moment, when our souls and spirits free themselves from our physical bodies, we can keep alive within us the living impulses of feeling, will, and concepts that are capable of further growth and that were implanted in our souls during childhood days. In that case, we not only remember experiences undergone at school but can relive them time and again, finding in them a source of ever-renewing life forces. Although, naturally, we grow old in limbs, with wrinkled faces and grey hair and possibly even suffering from gout, we will nevertheless retain a fresh and youthful soul and, even in ripe old age, one can grow younger again without becoming childish.

What some people, perhaps at the age of fifty, experience as a second wave of youthful forces is a consequence of the soul's having become strong enough, through education, to enable it to function well not only while it has the support of a strong physique but also when the time comes for it to withdraw from the body.

A teacher and educator must not only deal with the business of teaching actual subjects to pupils; she or he must also bear the burden of responsibility for their pupils' inner happiness and feeling of security right into the last years of their lives.

This is how we can foresee the consequences of what we are implanting in childhood through education and school lessons. But we can also follow the consequences in social life. Social morality is a kind of plant that has its roots in the classroom in which children were taught between their seventh and fourteenth years. And, just as a gardener will look at the soil of his garden, so society too should look at the "soil of the school," for the ground for morality and goodness is to be found here.

Anthroposophy seeks to be knowledge of human beings that is able to satisfy both individual and social life. It wishes to fructify the various fields of life. Hence, it also wants to fructify theory and practice in education.

In only two lectures, it is impossible for me to give more than just a few directives. Anthroposophy will continue to work further. What has been achieved so far regarding the foundations of pedagogy is only a modest beginning. In Dornach, at Christmas, I shall try to expand our anthroposophical pedagogy in a whole series of lectures, open to a wider international audience.[1] What I wished to show with the few guidelines that I have given here is that what matters most in anthroposophy is never a theory or a form of ideas leading to a certain conception of the world but practical life itself. This is certainly so in the field of education, although often it is unrecognized. Anthroposophy is often considered to be alienated from life. This, certainly, it does not want to be. Anthroposophy does not encourage adherents of spiritual knowledge to escape into "cloud cuckoo land," thus estranging them from life. It strives for spiritual knowledge so that the spirit can be experienced in all its creativity, at work in all material existence. That the spirit is creative can be seen in the as yet small successes of the Free Waldorf school in Stuttgart. Teaching our pupils is by no means the only task of the Waldorf school. Many subsidiary activities are pursued there as well. Whenever I can be there, we have staff meetings. At those meetings,

1. See Rudolf Steiner, *Soul Economy and Waldorf Education.*

almost every pupil is discussed individually, not just from the point of view of making judgments but very much from the point of view of how and what we can learn from the individuality of each child. Wonderful results have emerged from such discussions.

For a long time now, I have wondered how a majority of boys or of girls affects a class, for we have classes where boys are in the majority, others where girls predominate, and still others where the numbers of boys and girls are more or less balanced. It is never possible to predetermine, from personal contact with such classes, the effect of the relationships of boys to girls: imponderables play their part in the situation. But a class in which girls are in the majority is very different—neither better nor worse of course but all the same very different—from a class in which boys predominate. And, again, a class in which the numbers are more evenly balanced has a very different character. However, something has come into being, especially through working in our meetings with the progress of our pupils—something that is already outwardly expressed in the way we write our school reports. This is what one could call "the Spirit of the Waldorf school." When we talk about the school—I say this in all modesty—it is no longer enough to speak only about its twenty-five to twenty-eight teachers: it is also possible to speak about the Waldorf school spirit.

This Waldorf school spirit spreads its life and existence beyond the school, right into the pupils' families. For I know how happy those families are to receive our annual reports and with what happiness our children take them home. I do not wish to tread on anyone's toes. Please forgive me if I mention a personal idiosyncrasy—but I have never been able to discriminate correctly among the various grades or marks that are given, say between B- and B or the difference between a "nearly satisfactory" and a "satisfactory." In view of all the imponderables, I have always found it impossible to discern the differences that are indicated by such marks.

We do not make use of such marks in our reports. We simply describe the life of the pupil during the year, so that each report represents an individual effort by the teacher. We also include in each report a verse for the year that has been specially chosen for the individuality of the child in words with which she or he can live and in which he or she can find inner strength until the coming of a new verse at the end of the next school year. In that way, the report is an altogether individual event for the child. Proceeding thus, it is quite possible for the teacher to write some strong home truths into a report. The children will accept their mirror images, even if they are not altogether pleasing ones. In the Waldorf school, we have managed this not only through the relationship that has developed between teachers and pupils but also, above all, through something else that I could describe in further detail and that we can call "the spirit of the Waldorf school." This spirit is growing; it is an organic being. Naturally, I am speaking pictorially, but even such pictures represent a reality.

We are often told, "Not all teachers can be perfect. In education one can have the best principles, but they founder on human weaknesses." Yet, if the living spirit of which I speak, which issues from anthroposophical knowledge of human beings, exists and if we can respond to it in the right way, then, through it, the human being can grow and mature. I hope that I am not saying too much when I tell you that the teachers in the Waldorf school have greatly matured through the spirit of the Waldorf school. They are aware of it; they can feel its presence among them. They are growing and developing under its guidance. They can feel how many of their individual gifts, which contribute to the life of the Waldorf school, become independent, blending into a homogeneous spirit, and how that spirit is working in all teachers and educators, planting germs that can be of value for their pupils' whole lives in the ways that I have described. We can perceive it in various separate phenomena.

Naturally, we also have our share of less able children, and it has become necessary to separate some of them from their classmates. Hence, a very devoted teacher has organized a remedial class. Whenever a pupil is supposed to join the remedial class, his or her class teacher must endure a painful struggle, and no pupil is transferred to the remedial class except for the most urgent reasons. If we proceed merely by following a fixed scheme, many children would be sent into that special class, but a teacher often insists on keeping a child among his or her classmates, despite the great additional burdens that may be involved.

These are things that I mention not to boast but to characterize the situation. I would refrain from speaking about them were it not necessary to show that anthroposophy is capable of offering a sound pedagogical basis on which to deal with the realities of life—a pedagogical basis that leads to a spirit that will carry a human being without having to be carried, as is the case with an abstract form of spirit. This living spirit is what is needed in our decaying civilization. We should be able to consider each individual life problem within the context of life in general.

One problem, often called the most burning question of the day, is the so-called social question—it has drawn interest in the widest quarters. Apart from some positive aspects, this social question has also brought with it terrible misery—we only need to think of what is happening in Eastern Europe. It has many facets and one of these is doubtless that of education and teaching. One might even be justified in claiming that, without dedication to the question of education from the social point of view, out of insight into human nature, the social question, with all of its ramifications in the most varied areas of life, can hardly be put on a sound basis. Anthroposophy is anxious to deal honestly and seriously with all aspects of life and, above all, with education of the young.

Strangely enough, in our age of abstraction and intellectuality, a certain concept has been completely lost with regard to spiritual and cultural life. But, if we go back to ancient Greece, we still find it. According to that concept, learning and teaching are at the same time healing and health-giving processes. In ancient Greece, people were still aware that teaching made human beings healthy, that what is given as soul and teaching content creates a process of healing. During the Greek stage of human evolution, teachers also felt themselves to be healers in the widest sense of the word. Certainly, times are always changing and the character of human development changes too. Concepts cannot remain unaltered. We cannot today return to the concept of a sinful humanity, and see in the child, too, a sinful member of humanity whom we must heal. From that point of view, we could see in education only a kind of higher, spiritual medicine. However, we see the situation more correctly when we realize that, depending upon how we affect a child by our education, we create health-giving or illness-inducing effects in the child's soul, which certainly affect its physical condition as well.

It is with this in mind—that human beings may develop in healthy ways in spirit, soul, and body as far as this is possible within their given predispositions—that anthroposophical pedagogy and practice wishes to make its own contribution. Anthroposophy wishes to found educational principles and methods that have a healing influence upon humanity, so that what we give to the child and what we do in the proximity of the child, though not amounting to medicine in a restricted sense, nevertheless become a way of turning human life in a healing direction—as regards both the individual and the body social.

QUESTIONS AND ANSWERS

In connection with the first lecture, further clarification was sought in relation to raising the question of immortality with children aged nine to ten.

RUDOLF STEINER:
We are not dealing here with the question of immortality *per se* in an explicit sense. But I would like to say that this question is part of the complex life situation for children of that age. I don't think that I expressed myself unclearly when I said that at this age the child experiences a new form, a metamorphosis, in relation to the authority-based relationship of teacher to child. Previously, the child simply looked up to the teacher. This must be judged not on the basis of any party-political attitudes but on the basis of the child's development. Between the second dentition and puberty, a child can only feel, what my teacher says is what my soul must believe; what my teacher does is a commandment for me. After that period, when children see an example to be followed in their teachers, they become aware that their teacher, too, looks up to a higher authority. They feel dimly that authority is no longer to be found in this world, but has withdrawn into the divine-spiritual world. In short, what lives in the teacher's relationship to the supersensible world should not enter the feeling life of the child.

It is unlikely that a child will question the teacher regarding immortality in so many words. But the whole conduct of the child shows its dependence on the teacher's realizing that, through the authority that she or he wields, the child wishes to be brought into a relationship with the supersensible. How that is done depends on each individual case. One case hardly ever resembles another. For instance, it might happen that a child, after previously having been its usual cheerful self, enters school in a moody and morose condition that lasts for several days. If one has the necessary experience, one knows that such a brooding state is an outcome of the situation we have been discussing. Sometimes, there is no need for an explicit conversation about the reasons for the change in the child. The mere way in which the teacher relates to the child, the understanding way in which she or he talks lovingly to the child during such days of brooding, could itself lead the child across a certain abyss. It is not an abyss in an intellectual sense, but one connected with the general constitution of the child's soul. You will find the question of immortality there, not explicitly but implied. It is a question concerning the whole of life, one that will rise up in the child so that she or he can learn to feel, my teacher is not only an ordinary human being but one in whom the human relationship to the supersensible world is expressed. This is what I wished to add.

RUDOLF STEINER:
I have been given another question in writing which I should like to answer briefly. The question is: "Is it possible to follow the seven-year rhythms throughout the whole of life and what form do the various metamorphoses take?"

It is a fact that for those who are able to observe the more intimate changes of life, these rhythms are clearly identifiable during the early years of life; i.e., during the change of teeth and the onset of puberty. It is also easy to see that physical changes occur, paralleling those of soul and spirit. Such changing life-periods also exist in later life. They are less conspicuous and, strangely enough, become less distinctive as humanity progresses. I could also say that they become more inward. In view of our contemporary, more external ways of looking at history, it might not be inappropriate to mention that, in earlier stages of human evolution, such life periods were also clearly identifiable in later life. This is because human beings had different soul conditions in the past into which anthroposophy can look. I must add that anthroposophy is not dependent on documentary evidence as is modern historical research in our intellectual age. I am not blaming; I am merely describing. For instance, when we go back into earlier times, we notice how human beings looked forward to the coming of old age with a certain anticipation, simply on account of what they had experienced when they met other old people. This is a trait that one can discern if one looks back into human development without prejudice. Nowadays, people do not look forward to old age as a time when life will reveal certain things for which one is ready only then. That is because the clear distinctions between the various life periods have gradually been blurred. If we observe things without prejudice, we can perceive that we can today barely distinguish such development in most people beyond the ages of twenty-eight or thirty. After this period, in the majority of our contemporaries, the developmental periods become very indistinct. During the period called the Age of the Patriarchs, a time when people still looked up to old age, one knew that this period of ebbing life forces could still offer unique experiences to the human being. Although the body was becoming increasingly sclerotic, the soul was freeing itself more and more from the body. Very different indeed are the intimate experiences of the soul during the time of the body's ascending life forces from those undergone at the other end of life.

But this growing young once more in a body that is physically hardening, of which I spoke in the lecture, also gives old age a certain strength. And, if we look back to ancient times, we find this strength there. I believe that it was not for nothing that the ancient Greeks saw, in Homer above all but also in other poets, people who were creative at the time when their souls were freer from the physical body which was deteriorating. (I am not now speaking about whether there ever was such a person on earth as the one we call Homer.) Much of what we have of oriental wisdom, in the Vedas and, above all, in the philosophy of the Vedanta, has grown out of souls who were becoming younger in old age.

Naturally, progress with regard to human freedom would not be possible if distinctions between the different life periods did not become blurred. Yet, in a more intimate way, they do still exist today. And those who have achieved a certain self-knowledge know well how what someone might have experienced in their thirties, appears strangely metamorphosed in their fifties. Even though it still belongs to the same soul, it nevertheless appears in different nuances. Such nuances might not have a great deal of meaning for us today because we have become so abstract and do not perceive, by means of a more refined and intimate observation of life, what is spiritually real. Yet these metamorphoses, following each other, do exist nevertheless. Even if there seems little time for these intimate matters in our age with its social upheavals, a time will come when human beings will be observed adequately once more, for humanity would otherwise move towards its downfall and decay.

Why should the wish to advance to real observation of human beings be lacking? We have made very great progress indeed with regard to the observation of external nature. And whoever knows how plant and animal species have been explored in greatest detail and how thoroughly external facts are being observed will not think it impossible that the immense efforts and the enormously penetrating observations that have been showered upon the study of external nature will not one day be applied equally to the study of the human being. When and how this might eventually happen will have to be left open for the time being. In any case, it is correct to say that the art of education will advance to the extent to which a thorough observation of human beings and the metamorphoses of the various life periods in later life are being undertaken.

I would like to go back once more to what I said yesterday; namely, that whoever has not learned to pray in childhood is not in a position to bless in old age, for more than a picture was implied. Respect and devotion engendered in childhood are transmuted at a much later age into a force that has a healing effect on human environment—especially upon children—so that we can call it a force of blessing. A picture, such as that of folded hands, given in the ninth or tenth year of life, will turn into hands raised in blessing during the fiftieth or fifty-fifth year—such a truth is more than a mere picture: it shows the inner organic interrelationships during the course of a human life, which reveal themselves in such metamorphoses.

As I said before, these phases do become more blurred in later life. However, although they are less discernible, they do nevertheless exist, and they need to be studied, especially in the art of education.

7

Education and Drama

STRATFORD-ON-AVON — APRIL 19, 1922

Ladies and gentlemen! First, I would like to express my thanks to the "New Ideals in Education" Committee for inviting me to give two lectures during this Shakespeare Festival. Truly, it is no mere coincidence that I speak at this Shakespeare Festival and in German about the relationship of drama to education. For Shakespeare, the dramatist, through his dramatic works was a great educator and he was also a personality who, through his works, was of immense significance for the whole life of humankind. Indeed, in a sense, the connection of drama and education is historical through the fact that Shakespeare the dramatist was Goethe's teacher. Studying Goethe's biography not only factually but with the inner eye of a discerning spirit, we become aware that Goethe took from Shakespeare far more than the external features of dramatic form. Goethe drew from Shakespeare the whole educational spirit that he absorbed during the earlier years of his life. He mentioned three great teachers as having given direction to his life: Shakespeare, the botanist Linnaeus, and Spinoza the philosopher[1]—Linnaeus

1. William Shakespeare, 1564–1616; Carl von Linne, 1797–1788; Baruch Spinoza, 1632–1677, Dutch Philosopher.

because, at an early age, Goethe was opposed to the Linnaean conception of nature. From Spinoza Goethe could learn only an external manner of expression, philosophical language. From philosophy, Goethe could not learn his own *Weltanschauung,* his insight into inner necessity in nature and the universe; he learned it from works of art in Italy. His conception of the world was an artistic one. Spinoza gave him only the means of expressing it in philosophical terms.

However, in the inner configuration of his spirit, Goethe remained faithful to Shakespeare, even when he had passed, in his dramatic art, to a more antique tendency of form. It was thus Shakespeare who accompanied Goethe as an educator and guide throughout his life.[2]

Goethe's spirit can be linked inwardly to the spirit of Shakespeare. For Goethe himself described quite intimately how he allowed Shakespeare's spirit to work on him. Goethe liked to receive Shakespeare, not by seeing his plays acted on the stage, but by having them read to him in simple, quiet recitation. He would sit listening—his eyes closed—lifting himself out of the sphere of everyday intellectual life and sinking deeply into the fullness of his inner humanity. Such was the way in which Goethe wanted the Shakespearean spirit to enter into him.

In Dornach, we are endeavoring to work in the spirit of Goethe. The High School of Spiritual Science there, which has been founded by the anthroposophical world movement, has been given the name of the *Goetheanum*—not because I personally wished it so but above all (and this can be emphasized here) on account of the wishes of our English friends—because the Goethean spirit is to be cultivated in Dornach. At

---

2. For Goethe's view of Shakespeare, see "Shakespeare, A Tribute," and Shakespeare, Once Again" in *Goethe: Essays on Art and Literature* (NY: Shurkamp, 1986).

the Goetheanum, we are cultivating a direction in spiritual life that leads us to a definite understanding of new ideals of human education. We have been able to apply those ideals in practice at the Waldorf school in Stuttgart—a school closely linked to the High School of Spiritual Science in Dornach, to the Goetheanum. After the Great War, there was a great longing for the realization of spiritual-cultural life in Germany, and it became possible, through the initiative of Mr. Emil Molt, to found this Waldorf school in Stuttgart. It was my task to give methods of teaching and educational practices deriving from a deeper spiritual insight into human nature. I might perhaps be permitted to say a few words about the kind of spiritual knowledge that forms the background of the educational practices of the Waldorf school and that stems from the anthroposophical science being cultivated in Dornach.

I know that there are still a great many people in the world who believe that people are imbibing all sorts of fantastical illusions in Dornach, that some kind of cloudy mysticism is encouraged. But that is not the case at all. If we wish to judge the Dornach methods soundly, we must be ready to accept the fact that a really new direction in humanity's mental and spiritual life of humanity is being cultivated there. I would like to describe what we are doing by a word that is, I know, still very alarming to many people, inasmuch as all things of a supersensible nature do, after all, still alarm many people today. Nevertheless, I would like to speak this word openly and without reservations. The method applied in Dornach can be designated as "exact *clairvoyance*." It is not clairvoyance in the usual sense. What we understand by such clairvoyance does not arise pathologically from unknown depths of human nature but is developed and applied with scientific conscientiousness—a conscientiousness no less disciplined than what a scientist of external nature must cultivate in his or her scientific thought. To attain such "exact clairvoyance" and exercise it demands no less application of the human soul than is demanded of a mathematician or a practicing natural scientist. It is a clairvoyance that we apply consciously in matters of everyday life, a clairvoyance that awakens genuine faculties of knowledge and perception in the human soul. By these faculties, one becomes able to see beyond the things of the external world that have set their stamp on the civilization of the last three or four centuries. One becomes able to perceive the supersensible reality underlying the whole universe, all creation, and, above all, human nature.

Acquiring this kind of exact clairvoyance by a strictly methodical process, we become able to recognize and know what lives within us as a spiritual, supersensible reality between birth and death. When we are born into the world as little children, we appear to be only a physical organism. In reality—modern science might dispute it but this can become an absolute certainty by means of exact clairvoyance—a supersensible organism permeates the physical organism. It is an organism of forces. I have called it in my writings the "organism of formative forces." It consists simply of a configuration of forces—forces, however, that work inwardly.

This is the first supersensible reality to be seen and observed through exact clairvoyance. It is in no way connected with the old, unscientific concept of a life or vital force. Rather, it is something that enters the sphere of supersensible perception with the same clarity as colors and sounds do within the sphere of the ordinary sense perceptions of seeing and hearing.

Exact clairvoyance of the organism of formative forces is, however, only the first stage in supersensible cognition attained by a person who sees the supersensible inner human being at work in the physical organism between birth and death. A further stage leads to perception of the supersensible member of the human being that is present before the person descends from the spiritual world to unite with a physical body through birth. This is the supersensible human organism that passes again into the spiritual world at death, when the physical body and the body of formative forces, named above, both succumb to decay.

By the power of such spiritual seership, exact clairvoyance unites what otherwise is taken purely intellectually with a view of what is spiritual or supersensible in human beings. That is to say, it unites science and religion. On the other hand, it is also able to give a new impulse to the artistic element in life. For we cannot without it explain, in terms of such ordinary natural laws as we are accustomed to use in our treatment of external nature, the manner in which the supersensible organism—the body of formative forces—works on human beings between birth and death. This must be grasped and understood artistically. It is only by clairvoyantly raising the customary method of science to an artistic perception of the world that we can grasp how the forces that a person brings to earth and takes up into the spiritual world again organize him or her from birth until death.

Now, if we are working as teachers—as artists in education—on human beings, we must enter into relation with their supersensible, creative principle. For it is upon this principle that the teacher and educator works. External works of art can be created by fantasy and imagination. But, as an educator, one can be an artist only if one is able to enter into connection with the supersensible creative element, the supersensible that lives in the human being's self. The anthroposophical method of research makes this possible and so provides the basis for an art of teaching and education.

If we imagine a sculptor working at a figure that, when it is finished, comes to life and walks away, we can understand why the artist will count on his creation remaining as he or she leaves it. But, as parents and teachers, we are working on a child who not only lives on but grows and continues to evolve.

When educators have completed their work upon the child, they are in the position of an artist whose work continues to evolve. For this, philosophy does not suffice, only pedagogical principles and methods do: exact clairvoyance. I would like to sum up in a picture how we must work in such artistic education—for artistic education is, finally, the great principle of our Waldorf method. We know that a child's head, arms and legs continue growing and developing. The whole organism develops. Likewise, we must realize that the child before us is only in a childlike stage and that whatever we bring to the child—all that a child acquires through our education—goes on growing with the child throughout its life.

Waldorf education, which we at the Goetheanum are endeavoring to cultivate and carry into the world, sows in the child something that can grow and thrive from early childhood into old age. There are men and women who have a wonderful power in old age; they need only speak and the very tone of their voices, the inner quality of their speech, works as a blessing. Why, we might ask ourselves, can some people raise their hands and have an influence of real blessing? Our educational insight tells us that only those can do so who in childhood have learned to pray, to look up in reverence to another human being. To sum it up in one sentence, we can say that all children who rightly learn to fold their hands in prayer will be able to lift their hands in blessing in old age.

I would now like to speak about how we are trying to find the right pedagogy and educational practice.

Human life gives rise to many illusions. When speaking of the tasks of education, the greatest illusions are possible. We can proclaim wonderfully transparent ideals of education that appeal to heart and mind. We can even exercise persuasion with them—at first. But, in the real life of teaching and educating, something altogether different is needed from this faculty of knowing intellectually, or even in the goodwill of our hearts, what we wish to develop in the human beings we are educating. Imagine, for example, a teacher whose talents are not above average—for not every teacher can be a genius—and who must educate a child who will afterward become a genius. Very little of what such a teacher conceives as his or her ideals can be instilled into such a child. But a method of education founded on exact clairvoyance knows that there is an inmost core in the inner life of human beings and that the teacher or educator must simply prepare and smooth the way for this individual core. This inmost individuality always educates itself, through what it perceives in its surroundings, through what it receives by sympathy from life and from the situation into which life places it. Teachers and educators can work into this innermost individual core of the child only indirectly. What they must do is form and educate a child's bodily and soul life in such a way that, by the very nature of the education they provide, the growing child meets the minimum of hindrances and obstacles from the teacher's bodily nature, temperament, and emotional life.

Such an education can be achieved only if we really see how the human soul works in and on the body during these years of childhood. A child's inner bodily nature, when born into the world, is so organized that it may actually be described, strange as this might sound, as a kind of sensory organism. Until the change of teeth, which occurs around the seventh year, the whole child is one great sense organ. It receives impressions not only from the actions but also from the thoughts, feelings, and sentiments of those who educate it. Being thus surrendered to the environment, a small child is at the same time a little sculptor sculpting its whole human nature. It is wonderful to see this inner secret of the child's self-sculpture in the first seven years of its life (seven years, as I said, is only approximate—it continues until the change of teeth occurs).

How we speak to a child, whether we admonish it or not, the way we speak in a child's presence, the manner of our speech and of all our actions, all of this enters plastically into a child's inner life. This is the educative force. It is only an illusion to imagine that the child in those early years gains anything from our admonishments, our moral lecturing, our talking to it for its own good. In the presence of the child we should act, say, and think only what we would wish the child to receive into itself.

All of this changes when the child sheds its milk teeth, at approximately the age of seven—the exact moment is not to be taken pedantically. Around this time, the spiritual element that works plastically in the child grasps not only the nerve-and-sense system but also the lungs, the heart, and the circulatory system—the whole inner rhythm of the organism. In soul life, this spiritual element is connected with the life of feeling and fantasy. Thus, while we say that, until about the seventh year, the child is an inner sculptor, from then onward, until the fourteenth year—until the time of puberty—we can describe the child as an inner musician. We must not work on the child at this age with abstract concepts. We must realize that the child before us wants to permeate his or her whole body musically, with inner rhythm. We shall be educating the child rightly if we meet this inner rhythmical-musical need in the child. All education from the seventh to fourteenth years must thus be based upon an artistic approach to the subjects that are taught.

At first, the plastic and sculptural element is still at work. Writing and reading are taught, not abstractly, but deriving each letter from artistic feeling. Musical instruction is introduced and is widened out into eurythmy—which is, in effect, a rhythm of the whole organism. In eurythmy, the will for limb movements and the tendency to movement in the larynx and the neighboring speech organs is transferred to the whole body and its several movements. The larynx produces movements in the air, and thus to spoken sound. In eurythmy, the whole body becomes a moving organism of speech. We see the children take to eurythmy's language of movement with inner satisfaction, just as a small child takes to the spoken language of sound.

An artistic element underlies all teaching and education from the change of teeth till puberty. The artistic element is present also in what we are able to teach in the domain of art itself. At first, with the innate tendency to develop the plastic sense into an inner musical life, children are receptive to what we can bring by way of lyric poetry. Then, with the ninth or tenth year—earlier in one child, later in another—a sense for the epic awakens. We can now meet the child with epic poetry and poetic narrative. Then, at a quite definite moment in each child—approximately around the age of twelve—when sexuality is beginning to approach—we can observe how the child becomes receptive to the dramatic element. A demand awakens for what is dramatic. This is clearly evident if we perceive the child's development. Of course, this does not preclude teachers' having a dramatic element in themselves before this moment comes for the child. Indeed, teachers cannot cultivate eurythmy, nor lyric nor epic poetry, if they lack this dramatic element in their whole being. But it is from the age of about twelve that the child requires and needs the dramatic element in life.

This is the age, too, when we begin to make a transition from a purely artistic education to the first elements of intellectual education. Before this time, no importance should be attached to abstract concepts and intellectuality—in the teaching of nature study and natural science, for instance. Indeed, a person's whole life is marred if abstract concepts have been forced on them at too early an age during childhood. Before this twelfth year, everything that is taught should be based upon art and rhythm. But, with the twelfth year, we begin to introduce a certain element of the intellectual in our school—in the teaching of history, for example, inasmuch as history reveals the working of law; and, likewise, in the teaching of physics. And so it is now that, as an opposite pole to the intellectual element, the child demands dramatic activity.

In the Waldorf school at Stuttgart, where we are trying to work out of the child's nature in this manner, we have seen a group of boys of about thirteen or fourteen come and say, "We have been reading Shakespeare's *Julius Caesar*, and we would now like to act it, too." Thus, while we were careful to begin to develop intellectuality at the right age, young human nature asked for the element of drama of its own accord. This is what happens if we can bring children the right thing at the right time and in the right way. Naturally, the students said how pleased they were to have performed *Julius Caesar* and that this was of greater interest to them than watching a performance by professional actors on the stage. Nor can we wonder that it was Shakespeare who called forth this inner dramatic need in the boys of the Waldorf school. For we know that there is something in Shakespeare from which even Goethe could learn the essence of the dramatic. What lives in Shakespeare works into the soul and mind of the child, and becomes in the child a strong impelling force.

As the time is now well advanced, I should like to close for today. On Sunday, I shall have to speak again on Shakespeare in connection with the new ideals in education. Perhaps what I have had to say in a short talk on education and the role of drama may be a contribution to the endeavors of this honored educational society. Seeing, on the one hand, the world-historical figure of Shakespeare and on the other the great tasks of education, we cannot but be mindful that, while many ideals are necessary for our present life, the most important of them all will doubtless be the ideals of education.

RUDOLF STEINER'S NOTES

(for his lecture in Stratford on April 19, 1922)

I) It is an art of education, based on anthroposophy. It is different from other contemporary currents and world-views.

II) It depends on perceptions that can be developed.

Education: The free individuality of the child is not to be disturbed. We are to give the young human being an organism for life, which he or she can use properly. The soul will develop if we meet it with the right kind of human understanding. The spirit will find its way into the spiritual world. But the physical body is in need of education.

0–7th years. The human being develops from the head; the young child is entirely a sense organ and a sculptor.

The child under seven. Baby: sleeps a great deal because its whole body is like a sense organ—and every sense organ sleeps during the state of perceiving. The senses are awake when the human being is asleep. The secrets of the world lie in the senses; the secrets of the solar system lie in the chest organs. The senses are not predisposed for *perceiving*, but for plastically forming the organism.

7th–14th years. Human beings develop from the breathing and circulatory systems. A child is wholly a listener and a musician.

Learning to write—not too early—afterward learning to read—arithmetic—as analysis.

9th–10th years. Turning point. One can begin to talk about the outer world as the outer world—but through descriptions—*this* will harmonize the tendencies of growth.

In children, the soul exerts an immeasurably strong influence on the body.

14th–21st years. The human becomes a being of fantasy and of judgment. After the twelfth year, he or she can grow into the dramatic element. Something then remains for the rest of life. Before this time, a splitting of the personality is not good.

The question of "Drama and Education" has been raised in history through Goethe's relationship to Shakespeare.

1) The question of the relationship between drama and education will be answered by: What drew Goethe to Shakespeare?
2) Goethe mentions three teachers: Linnaeus, Spinoza, and Shakespeare. From the beginning, he stood in opposition to the first two. But he remained faithful to Shakespeare, although Goethe himself, in his dramatic works, comes to a different way of creating.
3) What attracted Goethe to Shakespeare was what escapes logical reasoning in Shakespeare. If one wanted to explain a Shakespeare play logically, one would be in the same position as someone wanting to explain dreams logically.

4) When is it right to introduce this element into education?

5) The Waldorf school is built on the artistic element. But teachers and educators arein a position different from other artists. They are not working with material that they can permanently shape; they are working with human beings.

6) The method of the Waldorf school is built on anthroposophy.

Exact clairvoyance. Exercises in thinking and willing.

Through these to recognize: the child—as sense organ and sculptor—and subsequently musician and listener to music.

7) Drama: the old Aristotelian definition: Fear and sympathy in tragedy. A human being facing something higher than the self. Satisfaction and gloating over other people's misfortunes. A human being facing a state of subordination.

8) In school, drama is to be introduced only at the time of puberty. But all teaching must pay attention to the dramatic element. The dramatic element escapes the intellect. Hence, it is employed as a counterbalance to the training of the pupils' intellectual powers.

Lyric poetry strengthens feeling—
epic poetry modifies thinking.

Consequently, a child's words become inward through lyricism. They become worldly through epic poetry.

Tragedy awakens mixed feelings: fear and sympathy.
Comedy awakens self-satisfaction and gloating over other people's misfortunes.

Comedy: The human being approaches the soul within.
Tragedy: The human being approaches the physical within.

Tasso and Iphigenia: are solutions to artistic problems
Faust: represents the problem of humanity

Shakespeare's characters are the creations of a theatrical pragmatist, created by someone who was in close and intimate contact with the audience. Goethe studies the problem of humanity in the single human being. Shakespeare embodies a certain kind of dreaming.

The impossibility for Sh. to find support in the outer arrangements of the stage. Hence, the interest is centered in the characters themselves.

In order to fully enjoy Shakespeare, Goethe outwardly contrives conditions bordering on dream conditions.

People always try to look for the logic in Shakespeare's plays. However, they are guided not by logic but by the pictorial element.

8

Shakespeare and the New Ideals

STRATFORD-ON-AVON — APRIL 23, 1922[1]

From the announcement of the theme of today's lecture "Shakespeare and the New Ideals," it might be expected that I would speak, above all, about new ideals. But I am convinced that it is not so necessary to speak of new ideals today as it is to speak of a wider question, namely the following: How are men and women of our time to regain the power to follow ideals? After all, no great power is required to speak about ideals; indeed, it is often the case that those who speak most about these great questions, expanding beautiful ideals in abstract words out of their intellect, are those who lack the very power to put ideals into practice. Sometimes, speaking of ideals amounts to no more than holding onto illusions in the mind in order to pass over life's realities.

At this festival, however, we have every cause to speak of what is spiritual as a reality. For this festival commemorates Shakespeare, and Shakespeare lives in what is spiritual in all that he created; he lives in it as in a real world. Receiving Shakespeare into our minds and souls might therefore be the very stimulus to give us men and women of today the power,

1. Many gaps exist in the notes to this lecture, but because of the lack of a shorthand version it was impossible to check it for accuracy.

the inner impulse to follow ideals, to follow real, spiritual ideals. We shall see our true ideals aright if we bear in mind how transitory many modern ideals have been and are, and how magnificently firm are many old ideals that still hold their own in the world by their effectiveness. Do we not see wide circles of believers in this or that religion, who base their innermost spiritual life and their inner mobility of spirit on something of the past, and gain from it the power of spiritual upliftment? And so we ask how is it that many modern ideals, beautiful as they are, and held for a while with great enthusiasm by large numbers of people, before long vanish as into a cloud, whereas religious or artistic ideals of old carry their full force into humanity not just through centuries but even through millennia?

If we ask this question, we are brought back repeatedly to the fact that, whereas our modern ideals are generally no more than shadow pictures of the intellect, the old ideals were garnered from real spiritual life, from a definite spirituality inherent in the humanity of the time. The intellect can never give human beings real power from the depths of their being. And, because this is so, many modern ideals vanish and fade away long before what speaks to us, through the old religious faiths, or through the old styles of art, from hoary antiquity.

Returning to Shakespeare with these thoughts in mind, we know that a power lives in his dramatic work that not only always gives us fresh enthusiasm but also kindles within us—in our imaginations, in our spiritual natures—our own creative powers. Shakespeare has a wonderfully timeless power and, in this power, he is modern, as modern as can be.

Here, from the point of view of the connection between human ideals and Shakespeare, I might perhaps call to mind what I mentioned last Wednesday, namely Shakespeare's deeply significant influence on Goethe. Countless books and treatises have been written on Shakespeare out of academic cleverness—exceptional cleverness. Taking all of the learned works on *Hamlet* alone, I think that one could fill library shelves that would cover this wall. But, when we seek to find what it was in Shakespeare that worked on such a man as Goethe, we finally come to the conclusion that absolutely nothing relating to that is contained in all that has been written in these books. They could have remained unwritten. All of the effort that has been brought to bear on Shakespeare stems from the world of the human intellect, which is certainly good for understanding facts of natural science and for giving such an explanation of external nature as we need to found for our modern technical achievements, but which can never penetrate what stands livingly and movingly before us in Shakespeare's plays.

Indeed, I could go further. Goethe, too, from this standpoint of intellectual understanding, wrote many things on Shakespeare's plays by way of explanation—on *Hamlet,* for example—and all of this, too, that Goethe wrote, is, in the main, one-sided and barren. However, what matters is not what Goethe said about Shakespeare, but what he meant when he spoke from his inmost experience, for example, when he said, "These are no mere poems! It is as though the great leaves of fate were opened and the storm-wind of life were blowing through them, turning them quickly to and fro."[2] These words are no explanation, but voice the devotion of his spirit. Spoken from his own humanity, they are very different from what he himself wrote by way of explanation about *Hamlet.*

Now, we might ask, why is it that Shakespeare is so difficult to approach intellectually? I shall try to give an answer in a picture. Someone has a vivid dream in which the characters

2. Actually Goethe wrote: "All Shakespeare's works are thus floating leaves from the great book of nature, chronicles and annals of the human heart."

enact a whole incident before the dreamer. Looking back on it later with the intellect, she or he might say that this or that figure in the dream acted wrongly; here is an action without motive or continuity, here are contradictions. But the dream cares little for such criticism. Just as little will the poet care how we criticize with our intellect and whether we find actions contradictory or inconsistent. I once knew a pedantic critic who found it strange that Hamlet, having only just seen the ghost of his father before him, should speak the monologue, "To be or not to be," saying in it that "no traveller returns" from the land of death. This, the man of learning thought, was really absurd! I do not mean to say that Shakespeare's dramatic scenes are dream scenes. Shakespeare experiences his scenes in full, living consciousness. They are as conscious as can be. But he uses the intellect only insofar as it serves him to develop his characters, to unfold them, to give form to action. He does not make his intellect master of what is to happen in his scenes.

I speak here from the anthroposophical view of the world. This view I believe, does contain the great ideals of humanity. Perhaps, therefore, I may mention at this point a significant experience that explains fully—by means of "artistic seership"—something that was first known through feeling. I have already had occasion to speak about the way in which "exact clairvoyance" is being cultivated at the Goetheanum, the school of spiritual science in Dornach, Switzerland. I have described the paths to this exact clairvoyance in the books translated into English as *How to Know Higher Worlds, Theosophy,* and *An Outline of Occult Science*. By means of certain exercises, carried out no less precisely than in the learning of mathematics, we can strengthen our soul faculties. Gradually, we can so develop our powers of thought, feeling, and will that we are able to live with our souls consciously—not in the unconsciousness of sleep or in dreams—outside the body. We become able to leave behind the physical body with its intellectualistic thought—for this remains with the physical body—in full consciousness. Then we have "imaginations," by which I do not mean such fanciful imaginings as are justified in artistic work, but I mean *true imaginations*, true pictures of the spiritual world surrounding us. Through what I have called "imagination," "inspiration," and "intuition," we learn to perceive in the spiritual world. Just as we consciously perceive this physical world and, through our senses, learn to build an understanding of it as a totality from the single sensory impressions of sound and color, so from the spiritual perceptions of exact clairvoyance we learn to build up an understanding of the spiritual world as a totality. Exact clairvoyance has nothing to do with hallucinations and illusions that enter a human being pathologically, always clouding and decreasing consciousness. In exact clairvoyance, we come to know the spiritual world in full consciousness, as clearly and as exactly as when we do mathematical work. Transferring ourselves into high spiritual regions, we experience pictures comparable, not with what are ordinarily known as visions, but rather with memory pictures. But these are pictures of an absolutely real spiritual world.

All of the original ideals of humanity in science, art, and religion were derived from the spiritual world. That is why the old ideals have a greater, more impelling power than modern intellectual ideals. The old ideals were seen in the spiritual world through clairvoyance, a clairvoyance that was at that time more instinctive and dreamlike. They were derived and taken from a spiritual source. By all means let us recognize quite clearly that certain contents of religious faith are no longer suited to our time. They have been handed down from ancient times. We need once more wide-open doors to look into the spiritual world and to take thence, not such abstract ideals as are spoken of on every side, but the power to follow the ideal and the spiritual in science, in art, and in religion.

If we approach Shakespeare with such powers of seeing into the spiritual world, we shall experience something quite specific, and it is of this that I wish to speak. Shakespeare can be understood with true and artistic feeling; exact clairvoyance is, of course, not necessary to have a full experience of his power. But exact clairvoyance can show us something most significant, which will explain why it is that Shakespeare can never let us feel he has left us, why it is that he is forever giving us fresh force and impulse. It is this: whoever has attained exact clairvoyance by developing the powers of thought, feeling, and will can carry over into the spiritual world what we have experienced here of Shakespeare. This is possible. What we have experienced here in the physical body—let us say that we have been entering deeply into the character of Hamlet or Macbeth—we can take this experience over into the spiritual world. We can see what lived in Shakespeare's deep inner life only when we compare it with the impressions that we are able to take over into the spiritual world from poets of more modern times. I do not wish to mention any particular poet by name—I know that everyone has his or her favorite poets—but any one of the naturalistic poets, particularly of recent years, could be mentioned. If we compare what we take over from Shakespeare with what we have in the spiritual world from these poets, we discover the remarkable fact that Shakespeare's characters live! When we take them over into the spiritual world, they act. They act differently, but they bring their life here into the spiritual world. Whereas, if we take over the characters created by a modern naturalistic poet into the spiritual world, they really behave more like dolls than human beings! They have no life in them at all, no movement!

Shakespeare's men and women keep their life and character. But the characters of many other poets, derived from naturalism, are just like wooden dolls in the spiritual world! They go through a kind of freezing process! Indeed, we ourselves are chilled by contact with such modern poetry in the spiritual world.

I am not saying this out of any kind of emotion, but as a matter of experience. With this experience in mind, we may ask again: what was it that Goethe felt? "It is as though the great book of fate is opened in Shakespeare, and life's stormy wind is turning its pages quickly to and fro." Goethe knew and felt how Shakespeare created from the full depths of the spiritual world. This has given Shakespeare his real immortality: this makes him ever new. We can go through a play of Shakespeare's and experience it ten, twenty, a hundred times!

Ladies and gentlemen, you have had before you within the last few days the scene from *Much Ado about Nothing* where the Friar kneels down beside the fallen heroine and utters his conviction of her innocence. It is something unspeakably deep and true, and there is hardly anything in modern literature to be compared with it. Indeed, it is most often the intimate touches in Shakespeare that work with such power and reveal his inner life and vitality.

Or again, in *As You Like It*, where the Duke stands before the trees and all of the life of nature in the Forest of Arden, and says that they are better counselors than those at court, for they tell him something of what he is as a human being. What a wonderful perception of nature speaks from the whole of this well known passage! "... tongues in trees, books in the running brooks...." Here is an understanding of nature, here is a reading of nature! It is true that the more modern poets can also indicate such things, but we often feel that in them it is something second-hand. In Shakespeare, we feel that he is himself everything. Even when they both say the same, it is altogether different whether Shakespeare says it or some other poet.

Thus the great question comes before us: how is it that, in Shakespeare, there is this living quality that is so intimately related to the supersensible? Whence comes the life in Shakespeare's dramas? This question leads us to see how Shakespeare, working as he did in the sixteenth and seventeenth centuries, was able to create something that still had living connections with the life of the most ancient drama. And this most ancient drama, as it speaks to us from Aeschylus, from Sophocles,[3] is in turn a product of the mysteries, those ancient cultic, artistic actions that derive from the most ancient, instinctive, inner spiritual knowledge. We can understand what inspires us so in true art, if we seek the origin of art in the mysteries.

If I now make some brief remarks on the ancient mysteries as the source of the artistic sense and artistic creative power, the objection can of course very easily be made that what is said on this subject from the standpoint of exact clairvoyance is unsupported by sufficient proof. Exact clairvoyance, however, brings us into touch not only with what surrounds us at the present day but also, most empathically, with the world of history, with the historical evolution of humanity, and of the universe. Those who follow the method that I have described in my books can themselves investigate what exact clairvoyance has to say upon the subject of the mysteries.

When speaking of the mysteries, we are looking back into very ancient times in human evolution, times when religion, art, and science did not yet stand separately, side by side, as they do today. Generally, people are insufficiently aware of the

3. Aeschylus, 525–456 BC author of (among others) the *Oresteia* and *Prometheus Bound*; Sophocles, 496–406 BC author of the *Oedipus* Trilogy, *Elektra, The Trojan Women,* etc.

changes—the metamorphoses—that art, religion, and science have undergone before reaching the separation and differentiation that they experience today. I will mention only one thing to indicate how, to some extent, modern anthroposophical knowledge brings us into contact again with older forms of true artistic life.

Across the centuries, the works of earlier painters—those, say, before the end of the thirteenth and during the fourteenth centuries—come down to us. We need only think of Cimabue.[4] Thereafter, something that has rightly held sway in modern painting enters into painting. This is what we call perspective. In the paintings in the dome of the Goetheanum in Switzerland, you can see how we are returning once again to the perspective which lies in the colors themselves—where we have a different feeling in the blue, the red, and the yellow. It is as though we were leaving the ordinary physical world: the third dimension of space ceases to have significance, and we work in two dimensions only.

Thus, a painter can return to a connection with the ancient instinctive spiritual experience of humanity. It is this possibility that modern anthroposophy seeks to give through all that I have said concerning exact clairvoyance.

Looking back at the life of ancient, instinctive clairvoyance, we find it connected equally with the artistic, the religious, and the scientific; that is, with the whole of the ancient form of knowledge. There was always an understanding for the union of religion, art, and science—which in those days meant a revelation of divine cosmic forces—in the mystery cults. Insofar as they were a manifestation of divine forces, the mystery cults

4. Bencivieni di Pepo, known as Cimabue (1240–1302). Italian painter, known to have worked in Rome, Pisa, and Assisi. Renowned as being at once the culminating artist in the medieval Byzantine style and the first modern artist.

entered deeply into humanity's religious feelings; insofar as they were already what we call today artistic—what we cultivate in art—they were the works of art for the people of that time. And, insofar as those ancient peoples were aware that true knowledge is gained, not by seeking it onesidedly through the head, but through the experience of the whole being, the ancient mysteries in their development were also mediators for human knowledge as it then was. Today, on the other hand, according to the modern view, knowledge can be acquired simply by taking ordinary consciousness—remaining as we are—and observing nature, forming concepts from the facts of nature.

Our modern way of approaching the world in order to gain knowledge of it is not the same as it was in ancient times. In the old way, to look into the spiritual world, one had to lift oneself to a higher level of one's humanity. Of course, this ancient way of knowing was not the same as our present exact clairvoyance. Nevertheless, the human being did see into the spiritual world. The mystery rites were enacted, not to display something for the outer eye, but to awaken inner experience in the whole human being. Mighty destinies formed the subject of these mystery rites. Through them, human beings were brought to forget their ordinary selves. They were lifted out of ordinary life. Although in a dream and not as clearly as is required today, they entered the state of living outside their bodies. That was the purpose of the mysteries. By the witness of deeply-moving scenes and actions, the mysteries sought to bring the neophyte to the point of living and experiencing outside the physical body.

There are certain fundamental experiences characteristic of life outside the body. One great experience is the following. In the physical body, our ordinary life of feeling is interwoven with the organic processes in our own body. But when we are outside the body, our feeling encompasses everything that surrounds us. We experience in feeling all of the life around us. Imagine that a person is outside the physical body with his or her soul and spiritual life and experiences spiritually—not with the intellect's ice-cold forces, but with the forces of the soul, with feeling and emotion. Imagine what it feels like to experience outside the body in this way. It is a great sympathy with all things—with thunder and lightning, with the rippling of the stream, the welling forth of the river spring, the sighing of the wind—and a feeling of togetherness also with other human beings, as well as with the spiritual entities of the world. Outside the body, one learns to know this great empathy.

Now, united with this great feeling of empathy, another fundamental feeling also comes over the human being in the face of what is at first unknown. I refer to a certain sense of fear. These two feelings—the feeling of empathy with all the world, and the feeling of fear—played a great part in the ancient mysteries. When the pupils had strengthened themselves in their inner lives so that they were able, without turning away and without losing their inner control, to bear both the living empathy with the world and the fear, then they were ripe enough and sufficiently evolved really to see into the spiritual worlds. They were then ready to live and experience the spiritual world. And they were ready, too, to communicate to their fellow human beings knowledge drawn from spiritual worlds. With their feeling, they could work down from the spiritual worlds into this world, and a new poetic power was revealed in their speech. Their hands became skilled to work in colors; they were able to command the inner rhythm of their organism so that they could become musicians for the benefit of other human beings. In this way, they became artists. They could hand down from the mysteries what the primeval religions gave to humanity. Anyone who looks into the Catholic Mass with inner spiritual knowledge knows that it is the last shadowlike reflection of what was living in the mysteries.

At first, what was living in the mysteries had its artistic and its religious side. Afterward, these two separated. In Aeschylus and in Sophocles we already see the artistic element, as it were, lifted out of the mysteries. There is the divine hero, Prometheus. In Prometheus, the human being comes to know something of the deeply-moving, terrifying experiences, the inner fear of the mysteries. What was living in the mysteries, in which the neophytes were initiated into a higher stage of life, becomes in Prometheus a picture, though permeated with living dramatic power. Thus drama became an image of the deepest human experiences. Aristotle, who was already, in a sense, an intellectual, still lived in some of the old traditions. He knew and experienced how drama was a kind of echo of the ancient mysteries. For this reason, Aristotle said, putting into words what was an echo of the ancient mysteries living on in Aeschylus and Sophocles, what has been dismissed by learned men again and again in their books: "Drama is the representation of a scene calling forth sympathy and fear, in order that human beings may be purified of physical passions, that they may undergo catharsis." We cannot understand what this catharsis, or purification, means unless we look back into the ancient mysteries and see how people were purified of what is physical and lived through mighty experiences in the supersensible, outside their physical bodies. Aristotle describes what had already become a picture in Greek drama. Afterward, this passed over to later dramatists, and we see in Corneille and Racine[5] something that is a fulfillment of Aristotle's words. We see characters clothed, as it were, in fear and compassion—

5. Great French classical tragedians: Pierre Corneille (1606–1684); Jean Baptiste Racine (1639–1699).

compassion that is none other than the ancient sympathy and experience with all the world that the human being experienced outside the body. The fear is always there when the human being faces the unknown. The supersensible is always, in a sense, the unknown.

Shakespeare entered into the evolution of drama in his time. He entered into a world that was seeking a new dramatic element. Something transcending ordinary human life lives in drama. Shakespeare entered deeply into this. He was inspired by that ancient dramatic power which, to a certain extent, was still felt by his contemporaries. And he worked in such a way that we feel in Shakespeare that more than a single human personality is at work: the spirit of his century is at work and, with it, the spirit of the whole of human evolution. Shakespeare still lived in that ancient feeling, and so he called something to life in himself that enabled him to form his dramatic characters and human figures, not in any intellectual way, but by living right within them himself. The characters of Shakespeare's plays come, not from human intellect, but from a power kindled and fired in the human being. It is this power that we must seek again if we would develop the true ideal of humanity.

Let us come back to the unification of art, science, and religion. This is our aim at the Goetheanum in Dornach. By the development of exact clairvoyance, we come to understand what was at work in the ancient mysteries. The element that the mystery dramatists placed, as yet externally, before their audiences was still at work in Shakespeare who recreated it in a wonderfully inward way.

It is no mere outer feature of Shakespeare's plays that we find in them about a hundred and fifty names of different plants and about a hundred names of birds, everywhere intimately, lovingly interwoven with human life. All of this is part of the single whole in Shakespeare.

Shakespeare took the continuous current that flows through human evolution from the ancient Mysteries—their cults and rites—wholly into his inner life. He took this impulse of the ancient mysteries and his plays come forth like dreams that are awake and real. The intellect with its explanations, its consistencies and inconsistencies, cannot approach them. As little as we can apply intellectual standards to a Prometheus or an Oedipus, just so little can we apply them to Shakespeare's plays.

Thus, in a wonderful way, we see in Shakespeare's own person a development that we can call a mystery development. Shakespeare comes to London where he draws on historical traditions for his material. In his plays, he is still dependent on others. We see then how, from about 1598 onward, a certain inner life awakens. Shakespeare's own artistic imagination comes to life. He is able to stamp his characters with the very interior of his being. Sometime later, when he has created *Hamlet*, a kind of bitterness toward the external physical world comes over him. We feel as though he were living in other worlds and judging the physical world differently—as though he were looking down from the point of view of other worlds. We then see him emerge from this inner deepening of experience with all of its inner tragedy. First, Shakespeare learns the external dramatic medium. Next, he goes through deepest inwardness—what I would call the meeting with the World Spirit, of which Goethe spoke so beautifully. Then he re-enters life with a certain humor, and his work carries with it the loftiest spirituality joined with the highest dramatic power. Here, I am thinking, for example, of *The Tempest*, one of the most wonderful creations of all humankind, one of the richest products of the evolution of dramatic art. In it, Shakespeare, in a living, human way, is able to lay his ripe philosophy of life into every character and figure.

So, having seen the art of drama derive from the ancient mysteries whose purpose was the living evolution of humanity, we can understand how it is that such an educational power goes out from Shakespeare's plays. We can see how Shakespeare's work, which arose out of a kind of self education given by nature herself, which he then lifted to the highest spirituality, can work in our schools and penetrate the living education of our youth. Once we have thus experienced their full cosmic spirituality, Shakespeare's dramas must be livingly present with us when we consider the great educational questions of the day. But we must be active with all of the means at our disposal, for only by the deepest spirituality shall we find in Shakespeare the answer to these questions.

Such are the ideals that humanity needs so sorely. We have a wonderful natural science in our time, but it places a world that is dense and material before us. It can teach us nothing else than the final end of it all in a kind of universal death. And, when we consider natural evolution, as it is given to us in the thoughts of the last centuries, it seems like something strange and foreign when we look up to our spiritual ideals. So we ask whether the religious ideal has a real force, adequate to the needs of the civilized world today. But it has not. We must regain this real force by rising to the spiritual world. Only then, by spiritual knowledge and not by mere belief, shall we find the strength in our ideals to overcome all material aspects in the cosmos. We must be able to lift ourselves up to the power that creates from truly religious ideals, the power to overcome the world of matter in the universe.

We can do this only if we yield ourselves to the spiritual conception of the world and, for this, Shakespeare can be a great leader. Moreover, it is an intense social need that there be a spiritual conception of the world working in our time. Do not think that I am speaking out of egotism when I refer once again to Dornach in Switzerland, where we are cultivating what can lead humanity once more into the reality of the spiritual, into the true spiritual nature of the world. Only because of this were we able to overcome many of those contending interests working in people today and so sadly splitting them into parties and differing sections in every sphere of life. I could mention that, from 1913 until now, almost without a break, through the whole period of the war, while nearby the thunder of the cannon was heard, members of no less than seventeen nations have been working together in Dornach. That seventeen nations could work together peacefully during the greatest of all wars, this, too, seems to me a great ideal in education. What is possible on a small scale should be possible on a large scale, and human progress—human civilization—needs it. And, precisely because we favor an international advance in human civilization, I point to Shakespeare as a figure who worked in all humanity. He gave all humanity a great inspiration for new human ideals, ideals that have a meaning for international, universal humanity.

Therefore, let me close on this festival day with these words of Goethe, words that Goethe was impelled to speak when he felt the fullness of the spirituality in Shakespeare. There then arose from his heart a saying that, I think, must set its stamp on all our understanding of the great poet, who will remain an eternal source of inspiration to all. Conscious of this, Goethe uttered these words on Shakespeare with which we may close our thoughts today:[6] "It is the nature of spirit to inspire spirit eternally." Hence, we may rightly say, "Shakespeare for ever and without end!"

---

6. These words were spoken by Goethe in a public address given by him on October 14th, 1771; printed in "Goethe's Works," Volume 41 of the Sophienausgabe *Literatur.*

9

Synopsis of a Lecture from the "French Course"

DORNACH — SEPTEMBER 16, 1922

Today is the time of intellectualism. The intellect is the faculty of soul, in the exercise of which our inner being participates least. We speak with some justification of the coldness of intellect, and we need only consider its effect on artistic perception or works of art. The intellect destroys or hinders. Artists dread the possibility that their creations might be conceptually or symbolically explained by clever reasoning. They would like their work to be understood with feeling, not with understanding. The soul warmth that gave their creations life disappears in such clarity; it no longer is communicated to the beholder. This warmth is repelled by an intellectual explanation.

In social life, intellectualism separates people from one another. We cannot work rightly within the community unless we are able to imbue our deeds, which always involve the weal or woe of our fellow human beings with a soul quality. Deeds alone, lacking soul, are not enough. In a deed springing from intellectualism, we withhold our soul nature, preventing it from flowing over to our neighbor.

It has often been said that intellectualism has a crippling effect in the teaching and training of children. In saying this, one is thinking, in the first place, only of the child's intelligence, not the teacher's. One would like to fashion the methods of teaching in such a way that not only the child's cold powers of reasoning are developed, but that warmth of heart may be engendered in the child as well.

The anthroposophical world-view is in full agreement with this. It accepts fully the excellent educational principles that have grown from this demand. But it realizes that warmth can be imparted only from soul to soul. Hence, it is of the opinion that, above all, pedagogy itself must become ensouled and thereby the teacher's whole activity too.

In recent times, indirectly influenced by modern science, teacher training has been strongly permeated by intellectualism. Parents have allowed science to dictate what is beneficial for a child's body, soul, and spirit; and so teachers, during their training, have received from science the spirit of their educational methods.

But science has achieved its triumphs precisely through intellectualism. It tries to keep its thoughts free from anything emanating from human soul life. Everything must come from sensory observation and experimentation. Such science could amass the excellent knowledge of nature in our times, but it cannot found a true pedagogy.

A true pedagogy must be based on a knowledge comprising the human body, soul, and spirit. Intellectualism grasps only the physical aspect of the human being, for only what is physical is revealed to observation and experiments. True knowledge of human beings is necessary before a true pedagogy can be founded. This is what anthroposophy seeks to attain.

One cannot come to knowledge of human beings by first forming an idea of the bodily nature with the help of a science founded merely on what can be grasped by the senses, and then asking whether that bodily nature is ensouled, and whether a spiritual element is active within it. In dealing with a child, such an attitude is harmful; for here, far more than in the adult, body, soul, and spirit form a unity. One cannot care first for the health of a child from the point of view of a merely natural science, and then want to give to the healthy organism what one regards as proper from the point of view of soul and spirit. In all that one does to and with the child, one either benefits or injures his bodily life. In earthly life, the human soul and spirit express themselves through the body. A bodily process is a revelation of soul and spirit.

Material science is necessarily concerned with the body as a physical organism. It does not reach an understanding of whole human beings. Many people feel the truth of this but, in regard to pedagogy, they fail to see what is actually needed today. They do not *say*: pedagogy cannot thrive on material science; let us therefore found our teaching methods on pedagogical instincts, not on material science. But they are half-consciously of this opinion.

We can admit this in theory but, in practice, because modern humanity has mostly lost the spontaneity of the life of instinct, it leads to nothing. It would be groping in the dark to try to construct a pedagogy on instincts that are no longer present in humanity in their original force. We come to see this through anthroposophical knowledge. We learn to know that the intellectualistic trend in science owes its existence to a necessary phase in the evolution of humanity. In recent times, people passed beyond the period of instinctive life. The intellect then became of predominant significance. Human beings had to advance along the evolutionary path in the right way. Just as an individual must acquire particular capabilities at a particular period of life, the evolutionary path led human beings to the level of consciousness that had to be attained in a certain epoch. The instincts are now crippled under the influence of the intellect, and yet one cannot try to return to the instinctive life without working *against* human evolution. We must accept the significance of the enhanced consciousness we attained through intellectualism, and give human beings—in full consciousness—what instinctive life can no longer give them.

To this end, knowledge of soul and spirit is needed, founded as firmly on spiritual reality as material, intellectualistic science is founded on physical reality. Anthroposophy strives for just this, yet it is just this that many people shrink from accepting. They learn to know how modern science tries to understand human nature. They feel that the modern scientific way is impossible, but they will not accept that, in order to attain knowledge of soul and spirit, it is possible to cultivate a new mode of cognition that is as clear in consciousness as that with which we penetrate physical phenomena. This being so, they want to return to the instincts as a way of understanding and training children.

But we must move forward; and there is no other way than to extend anthropology by knowledge of anthroposophy—to extend sensory knowledge by acquiring spiritual knowledge. We must learn all over again. People are terrified at the complete change of thought required for this. Out of unconscious fear, they attack anthroposophy as fantastic, yet anthroposophy wants only to proceed in the spiritual domain as soberly and as carefully as material science does in the physical.

Let us consider the child. At about the seventh year of life, a child develops his or her second teeth. This is not merely the work of the period of time immediately preceding this change. It is a process that begins with embryonic development and only concludes with the second teeth. These forces, which produce the second teeth at a certain stage of development, were always active in the child's organism. But they do not reveal themselves in this way in subsequent periods of life. Further tooth formations do not occur. And yet the forces concerned have not been lost, they continue to work, they have merely been *transformed.* They have undergone a metamorphosis (there are other forces, too, in the child's organism that undergo a similar metamorphosis).

If we study the development of the child's organism in this way, we discover how these forces (leading to the change of teeth) were previously active in the processes of nourishment and growth. They lived in undivided unity with the child's body, freeing themselves from it only around the seventh year. After the change of teeth, then, they live on as soul forces, active in older children in feeling and thinking.

Anthroposophy reveals that an etheric organism permeates the physical organism of the human being. Up to the age of seven, the whole of this etheric organism is active in the physical body. But a portion of it is now freed from direct activity in the physical body and acquires a certain independence as a vehicle for a soul life that is relatively free of the physical organism.

In earthly life, however, soul experience can develop only with the help of the etheric organism. Before the age of seven years, the soul is quite embedded in the physical body and expresses itself actively only through the body. The child can enter into relationship with the outer world only when this relationship takes the form of a stimulus that runs its course within the body. This can happen only when the child *imitates.* Before the change of teeth, the child is, in the widest sense, a purely imitative being. The aim of education at this stage can therefore be expressed thus: *the conduct of those around the child should be worthy of imitation.*

A child's educators should experience within themselves what it is to have the whole etheric organism within the physical. This gives them knowledge of the child. One can do nothing with abstract principles alone. Educational practice requires an anthroposophical art of education to work out in detail how, through childhood, a human being gradually emerges.

Just as the etheric organism is embedded in the physical organism until the change of teeth, so, from the change of teeth until puberty, a soul organism, called by anthroposophy the astral organism, is embedded in the physical and etheric organism. As a result, the child develops a life that no longer expends itself in imitation. However, children of this age cannot govern their relation to others in accordance with fully conscious thoughts, regulated by intellectual judgment. This becomes possible only when, at puberty, a part of the soul organism frees itself from the corresponding part of the etheric organism. From the age of seven to the age of fourteen, the child's relationship is not determined by independent judgment. It is the relationship effected through authority that is important now.

This means that, during these years, children should look up to someone whose authority they can accept as a matter of course. The whole education must be fashioned with reference to this. One cannot build on children's powers of intellectual judgment at this age. One should perceive clearly that children want to accept what is put before them as true, good, and beautiful because their teachers, whom they take as their models, regard it as true, good, and beautiful.

Moreover, teachers must work in such a way that they do not merely put before the child the true, the good, and the beautiful, but, in a sense, they themselves *must be* these. Not so much what they *teach* but what the teachers *are* is what passes over into the children. Everything that is taught should be presented to the children not as a matter of theory but as a realizable ideal, as a work of art.

Bibliography

Books by Rudolf Steiner:

Anthroposophy and the Inner Life (Original English language title: *Anthroposophy—An Introduction*). Rudolf Steiner Press, Bristol, England, 1994.

The Apocalypse of St. John. Rudolf Steiner Press, London, 1977.

The Archangel Michael: His Mission and Ours. Anthroposophic Press, Hudson, NY, 1994.

The Boundaries of Natural Science. Anthroposophic Press, Spring Valley, NY, 1983.

The Case for Anthroposophy. Rudolf Steiner Press, London, 1970.

The Constitution of the School of Spiritual Science. Anthroposophical Society in Great Britain, London, 1964.

The East in the Light of the West. Spiritual Science Library, Blauvelt, NY, 1986.

Egyptian Myths and Mysteries. Anthroposophic Press, Hudson, NY, 1971.

Goethean Science. Mercury Press, Spring Valley, NY, 1988.

Goethe's World View Mercury Press, Spring Valley, NY, 1985.

How to Know Higher Worlds: A Modern Path of Initiation. Anthroposophic Press, Hudson, NY, 1994.

An Introduction to Eurythmy. Anthroposophic Press, Hudson, NY, 1984.

Intuitive Thinking as a Spiritual Path: A Philosophy of Freedom. Anthroposophic Press, Hudson, NY, 1995.

Life Between Death and Rebirth. Anthroposophic Press, Hudson, NY, 1968.

An Outline of Occult Science. Anthroposophic Press, Spring Valley, NY, 1972.

The Presence of the Dead on the Spiritual Path. Anthroposophic Press, Hudson, NY, 1990.

The Renewal of the Social Organism. Anthroposophic Press, Spring Valley, NY, 1985.

The Riddles of Philosophy. Anthroposophic Press, Spring Valley, NY, 1973.

A Road to Self Knowledge and The Threshold of the Spiritual World. Rudolf Steiner Press, London, 1975.

Rudolf Steiner: An Autobiography . Steinerbooks, Blauvelt, NY, 1977.

The Social Future. Anthroposophic Press, Spring Valley, NY, 1972.

Science of Knowing (*The Theory of Knowledge Implicit in Goethe's World Conception*) Mercury Press, Spring Valley, NY, 1988.

Soul Economy and Waldorf Education. Anthroposophic Press, Spring Valley, NY, 1986.

Spiritual Beings in the Heavenly Bodies & in the Kingdoms of Nature. Anthroposophic Press, Hudson, NY, 1992.

Spiritual Science and Medicine. Steinerbooks, Blauvelt, NY, 1989.

The Stages of Higher Knowledge. Anthroposophic Press, Spring Valley, NY, 1967.

Theosophy: An Introduction to the Spiritual Processes in Human Life and in the Cosmos. Anthroposophic Press, Hudson, NY, 1994.

Turning Points in Spiritual History. Spiritual Science Library, Blauvelt, NY, 1987.

Books by other Authors:

Barnes, John, ed., *Nature's Open Secret: Rudolf Steiner and Goethe's Participatory Approach to Science.* Anthroposophic Press, Hudson, NY, forthcoming.

Bockemühl, J. and others. *Toward a Phenomenology of the Etheric World.* Anthroposophic Press, Spring Valley, NY, 1985.

Easton, Stewart. *Man and World in the Light of Anthroposophy* . Anthroposophic Press, Hudson, NY, 1989.

Easton, Stewart. *Rudolf Steiner: Herald of a New Epoch.* Anthroposophic Press, Hudson, NY, 1980.

Koepke, Hermann. *Encountering the Self.* Anthroposophic Press, Hudson, NY, 1989.

Lytton, Sir Edward Bulwer. *Zanoni: A Rosicrucian Tale.* Spiritual Literature Library, Blauvelt, NY, 1989.

McDermott, Robert A. *The Essential Steiner.* Harper Collins, San Francisco, 1984.

Raab, Rex; Klingborg, Arne; Fant, Åke. *Eloquent Concrete: How Rudolf Steiner Employed Reinforced Concrete.* Rudolf Steiner Press, London, 1979.

Publisher's Note Regarding Rudolf Steiner's Lectures

The lectures contained in this volume have been translated from the German edition, which is based on stenographic and other recorded texts that were in most cases never seen or revised by the lecturer. Hence, due to human errors in hearing and transcription, they may contain mistakes and faulty passages. We have made every effort to ensure that this is not the case. Some of the lectures were given to audiences more familiar with anthroposophy; these are the so-called "private" or "members" lectures. Other lectures, like the written works, were intended for the general public. The difference between these, as Rudolf Steiner indicates in his *Autobiography*, is twofold. On the one hand, the members' lectures take for granted a background in and commitment to anthroposophy; in the public lectures this was not the case. At the same time, the members' lectures address the concerns and dilemmas of the members, while the public work speaks directly out of Steiner's own understanding of universal needs. Nevertheless, as Rudolf Steiner stresses: "Nothing was ever said that was not solely the result of my direct experience of the growing content of anthroposophy. There was never any question of concessions to the prejudices and preferences of the members. Whoever reads these privately printed lectures can take them to represent anthroposophy in the fullest sense. Thus it was possible without hesitation—when the complaints in this direction became too persistent—to depart from the custom of circulating this material 'for members only.' But it must be born in mind that faulty passages do occur in these reports not revised by myself." Earlier in the same chapter, he states: "Had I been able to correct them [the private lectures] the restriction *for members only* would have been unnecessary from the beginning."

THE FOUNDATIONS OF WALDORF EDUCATION

THE FIRST FREE WALDORF SCHOOL opened its doors in Stuttgart, Germany, in September, 1919, under the auspices of Emil Molt, the Director of the Waldorf Astoria Cigarette Company and a student of Rudolf Steiner's spiritual science and particularly of Steiner's call for social renewal.

It was only the previous year—amid the social chaos following the end of World War I—that Emil Molt, responding to Steiner's prognosis that truly human change would not be possible unless a sufficient number of people received an education that developed the whole human being, decided to create a school for his workers' children. Conversations with the Minister of Education and with Rudolf Steiner, in early 1919, then led rapidly to the forming of the first school.

Since that time, more than six hundred schools have opened around the globe—from Italy, France, Portugal, Spain, Holland, Belgium, Great Britain, Norway, Finland and Sweden to Russia, Georgia, Poland, Hungary, Rumania, Israel, South Africa, Australia, Brazil, Chile, Peru, Argentina, Japan etc.—making the Waldorf School Movement the largest independent school movement in the world. The United States, Canada, and Mexico alone now have more than 120 schools.

Although each Waldorf school is independent, and although there is a healthy oral tradition going back to the first Waldorf teachers and to Steiner himself, as well as a growing body of secondary literature, the true foundations of the Waldorf method and spirit remain the many lectures that Rudolf Steiner gave on the subject. For five years (1919–24), Rudolf Steiner, while simultaneously working on many other fronts, tirelessly dedicated himself to the dissemination of the idea of Waldorf education. He gave manifold lectures to teachers, parents, the general public, and even the children themselves. New schools were founded. The Movement grew.

While many of Steiner's foundational lectures have been translated and published in the past, some have never appeared in English, and many have been virtually unobtainable for years. To remedy this situation and to establish a coherent basis for Waldorf Education, Anthroposophic Press has decided to publish the complete series of Steiner lectures and writings on education in a uniform series. This series will thus constitute an authoritative foundation for work in educational renewal, for Waldorf teachers, parents, and educators generally.

RUDOLF STEINER'S LECTURES (AND WRITINGS) ON EDUCATION

I. *Allgemeine Menschenkunde als Grundlage der Pädagogik. Pedagogischer Grundkurs,* 14 Lectures, Stuttgart, 1919 (GA293). ***The Study of Man*** (Rudolf Steiner Press, 1981).

II. *Erziehungskunst Methodische-Didaktisches,* 14 Lectures, Stuttgart, 1919 (GA294). ***Practical Advice to Teachers*** (Rudolf Steiner Press, 1988).

III. *Erziehungskunst,* 15 Discussions, Stuttgart, 1919 (GA 295). ***Discussions with Teachers*** (Rudolf Steiner Press, 1992).

IV. *Die Erziehungsfrage als soziale Frage,* 6 Lectures, Dornach, 1919 (GA296). ***Education as a Social Problem*** (Anthroposophic Press, 1969).

V. *Die Waldorf Schule und ihr Geist,* 6 Lectures, Stuttgart and Basel, 1919 (GA 297). ***The Spirit of the Waldorf School*** (Anthroposophic Press, 1995).

VI. *Rudolf Steiner in der Waldorfschule, Vorträge und Ansprachen,* Stuttgart, 1919–1924 (GA 298). ["**Rudolf Steiner in the Waldorf School—Lectures and Conversations,**" Stuttgart, 1919–24].

VII. *Geisteswissenschaftliche Sprachbetrachtungen,* 6 Lectures, Stuttgart, 1919 (GA 299). ***The Genius of Language*** (Anthroposophic Press, 1995).

VIII. *Konferenzen mit den Lehren der Freien Waldorfschule 1919–1924,* 3 Volumes (GA 300). ***Conferences with Teachers*** (Steiner Schools Fellowship, 1986, 1987, 1988, 1989).

IX. *Die Erneuerung der Pädagogisch-didaktischen Kunst durch Geisteswissenschaft,* 14 Lectures, Basel, 1920 (GA 301). ***The Renewal of Education*** (Kolisko Archive Publications for Steiner Schools Fellowship Publications, Michael Hall, Forest Row, East Sussex, UK, 1981).

X. *Menschenerkenntnis und Unterrichtsgestaltung,* 8 Lectures, Stuttgart, 1921 (GA 302). ***The Supplementary Course—Upper School*** (Michael Hall School, Forest Row, 1965) and ***Waldorf Education for Adolescence*** (Kolisko Archive Publications for Steiner Schools Fellowship Publications, 1980).

XI. *Erziehung und Unterrricht aus Menschenerkenntnis,* 9 Lectures, Stuttgart, 1920, 1922, 1923 (GA302a). The first four lectures available as ***Balance in Teaching*** (Mercury Press, 1982); last three lectures as ***Deeper Insights into Education*** (Anthroposophic Press, 1988).

XII. *Die Gesunder Entwickelung des Menschenwesens,* 16 Lectures, Dornach, 1921–22 (GA303). ***Soul Economy and Waldorf Education*** (Anthroposophic Press, 1986).

XIII. *Erziehungs- und Unterrichtsmethoden auf Anthroposophische Grundlage,* 9 Public lectures, various cities, 1921–22 (GA304). ***Waldorf Education and Anthroposophy I*** (Anthroposophic Press, 1995).

XIV. *Anthroposophische Menschenkunde und Pädagogik,* 9 Public lectures, various cities, 1923–24 (GA304a). ***Waldorf Education and Anthroposophy II*** (Anthroposophic Press, 1995).

XV. *Die geistig-seelischen Grundkräfte der Erziehungskunst,* 12 Lectures, 1 Special Lecture, Oxford 1922 (GA 305). ***The Spiritual Ground of Education*** (Garber Publications, n.d.).

XVI. *Die pädagogisch Praxis vom Gesichtspunkte geisteswissenschaftliche Menschenerkenntnis,* 8 Lectures, Dornach, 1923 (GA306). ***The Child's Changing Consciousness and Waldorf Education*** (Anthroposophic Press, 1988).

XVII. *Gegenwärtiges Geistesleben und Erziehung,* 4 Lectures, Ilkeley, 1923 (GA307). ***A Modern Art of Education*** (Rudolf Steiner Press, 1981) and ***Education and Modern Spiritual Life*** (Garber Publications, n.d.).

XVIII. *Die Methodik des Lehrens und die Lebensbedingungen des Erziehens,* 5 Lectures, Stuttgart, 1924 (GA308). ***The Essentials of Education*** (Rudolf Steiner Press, 1968).

XIX. *Anthroposophische Pädagogik und ihre Voraussentzungen,* 5 Lectures, Bern, 1924 (GA 309). ***The Roots of Education*** (Rudolf Steiner Press, 1982).

XX. *Der pädagogische Wert der Menschenerkenntnis und der Kulturwert der Pädagogik,* 10 Public lectures, Arnheim, 1924 (GA310). ***Human Values in Education*** (Rudolf Steiner Press, 1971).

XXI. *Die Kunst des Erziehens aus dem Erfassen der Menschenwesenheit,* 7 Lectures, Torquay, 1924 (GA311). ***The Kingdom of Childhood*** (Anthroposophic Press, 1995).

XXII. *Geisteswissenschaftliche Impulse zur Entwicklung der Physik. Erster naturwissenschaftliche Kurs: Licht, Farbe, Ton—Masse, Elektrizität, Magnetismus,* 10 Lectures, Stuttgart, 1919–20 (GA 320). ***The Light Course*** (Steiner Schools Fellowship,1977).

XXIII. *Geisteswissenschaftliche Impulse zur Entwickelung der Physik. Zweiter naturwissenschaftliche Kurs: die Wärme auf die Grenze positiver und negativer Materialität,*14 Lectures, Stuttgart, 1920 (GA 321). ***The Warmth Course*** (Mercury Press, 1988).

XXIV. *Das Verhältnis der verschiedenen naturwissenschaftlichen Gebiete zur Astronomie. Dritter naturwissenschaftliche Kurs: Himmelskunde in Bezeiehung zum Menschen und zur Menschenkunde,* 18 Lectures, Stuttgart, 1921 (GA 323). Available in typescript only as "**The Relation of the Diverse Branches of Natural Science to Astronomy**."

XXV. Miscellaneous.

Index

DURING THE LAST TWO DECADES of the nineteenth century the Austrian-born Rudolf Steiner (1861–1925) became a respected and well-published scientific, literary, and philosophical scholar, particularly known for his work on Goethe's scientific writings. After the turn of the century he began to develop his earlier philosophical principles into an approach to methodical research of psychological and spiritual phenomena.

His multifaceted genius has led to innovative and holistic approaches in medicine, science, education (Waldorf schools), special education, philosophy, religion, economics, agriculture (Biodynamic method), architecture, drama, new arts of eurythmy and speech, and other fields. In 1924 he founded the General Anthroposophical Society, which today has branches throughout the world.